PRAISE FOR RIDING THE DOG

"*Riding the Dog* is a beautiful, loving, and lovely story, filled with generous detail and heartfelt emotion. Jan Groft writes clearly, simply, and with wholehearted intelligence, resulting in this stunning tribute to father, family, and faith."

Dinty W. Moore, author of *The Accidental Buddhist*

"*Riding the Dog* is more than a beautiful book. It is a gift and a life companion. Its pages are incandescent and rock-ribbed with wisdom, compassion, and faith. Jan Groft is a writer of extraordinary courage and grace. Her work floods the darkest corners of human existence with a pure and sanctifying light. In its unflinching look at dying, *Riding the Dog* teaches us how to live."

Susan Dodd, author of *The Mourners' Bench*

"Every page of *Riding the Dog* radiates with eloquent anguish and the tender precision of one who has not only been harrowed by her father's downward spiral into death but who possesses the tenacious spirit and literary gifts to be able to convert this chaos into meaning, and to see the spiral, ultimately, climbing upward."

Christopher Noël, author, *In the Unlikely Event of a Water Landing: A Geography of Grief*

"Jan Groft is a fine writer who stirs the heart and spirit, reminding us that love does not end with death."

Kate Young Caley, author of *The House Where The Hardest Things Happened*

Riding the dog

My Father's Journey Home

Riding the dog

My Father's Journey Home

a memoir
jan groft

FaithWalk
PUBLISHING

Grand Haven, Michigan

Published by FaithWalk Publishing
Grand Haven, Michigan 49417

Scripture quotations, unless otherwise indicated, are taken from the HOLY BIBLE, NEW INTERNATIONAL VERSION®. NIV®. Copyright © 1973, 1978, 1984 by International Bible Society. Used by permission of Zondervan. All rights reserved.

The author thanks *Central PA* Magazine and publisher WITF, Inc. for permission to reprint a portion of her essay entitled "Breathing for Elaine," which appeared in the August, 1998 edition of that publication.

Printed in the United States of America

09 08 07 06 05 04   7 6 5 4 3 2 1

Library of Congress Cataloging-in Publication Data

Groft, Jan.
    Riding the dog : my father's journey home : a memoir / Jan Groft
        p. cm.
    ISBN 1-932902-41-4   (pbk. : alk. paper)
    1. Fathers--Religious life.
    2. Fathers and daughters--Religious aspects--Christianity. I. Title.
    BV4846.G76 2004
    277.3'083'0922--dc22
                            2004006579

*In memory of my father,
this book is dedicated to
his grandchildren.
May you all keep the spirit alive.*

ACKNOWLEDGMENTS

Many people have contributed to the shaping of this book. What a gift it has been to work with them and to have them in my life.

Mildred Lorch and Dinty W. Moore read an early manuscript of this book. Their wisdom and thoughtful insights spurred this project on.

Peg and David Marks and Howard Rice held my hand and my heart in friendship. I am forever learning from them and forever inspired by their genuineness.

My sisters, Marge Henderson, Pat Latshaw, and the late Lena Baleno and Dolores McGreevy, have been fun and lively traveling companions on the road to finding out who we are and why.

My niece Janice Brickley chalked up sales of this book before I was finished writing it. She also provided the old family photo for the cover.

Dirk Wierenga and Louann Werksma at FaithWalk took the chances that made the difference. Their guidance was invaluable. Ginny McFadden provided capable production assistance.

Katherine Groft was a champion of and believer in this project from day one. I hope she will always remember: "I love you all the way up to the sky and back again."

Randy Groft, my husband, friend, and artist-in-residence, generously provided his incomparable design talent and his gentle listening.

I am especially grateful to my heavenly Father for providing all the words on these pages plus encouragement, such as this: "Blessed is she who has believed that what the Lord has said to her will be accomplished." (Luke 1:45)

J.G.
April, 2004

Author's Note

Some names and identifying traits of the people who appear on these pages have been changed.

As they were walking along
and talking together,
suddenly a chariot of fire
and horses of fire appeared
and separated the two of them,
and Elijah went up
to heaven in a whirlwind.

(2 Kings 2:11)

1

Nobody Lives Forever

My father is in my sunroom dying. You cannot tell me that God did not script this scene. Ceiling fan twirling in rhythm to the oxygen concentrator, chugging, spitting, chugging, spitting. Five arched windows, each with twenty panes, frame a close-up of Armstrong pines. Hollyhocks inch toward their second bloom: blood reds, pinks, peaches. Renovations to this room, formerly my husband's graphic design studio, were completed barely three months ago. Built-in desks ripped out, computers and printers relocated, fax and photocopier removed just in time to accommodate, unbeknownst to us, a divine schedule for set design: a Turkish rug—periwinkle, salmon and tan—a striped, deep-seat sofa with floral cushions, matching ottoman, and two new chairs, one for the hospice nurse to keep watch through the night shift, the other for us to take turns sitting next to Dad and holding his hand.

Though no one could care less about the stylishness of his bed sheets, there he is, my father, exhaling the way a fire smolders, behind him a layered palette of plaids and florals, stripes and chambrays. Nearby a towel is draped over the face of a grandmother's clock, its hands stilled to silence its chimes. The clock's face is hidden to keep Dad—and the rest of us—from thinking that time has stopped at 1:50.

Dad's hand, cupped like the shell of a walnut, rests inside mine against a pattern of yellow and pink peonies on an aqua background. His hand is pale and old, traits I have never associated with my father. I cannot remember a time when he did not have a tan, always looking as if he had just come from the golf course. In one way, it is now difficult to imagine this same hand waving hello to my seven-year-old daughter, Katherine, and me three months ago, as Dad and Mother descended the airplane's narrow stairway upon their arrival in Lancaster. In another way, the moment is as vivid as if it were just now unfolding outside my sunroom window.

Hello, Honey, says the glimmer in his eyes, as he spots Katherine and me waving at him from the terminal window. His white, wavy hair is cropped short and tidy. A black brief-case dangles from his other hand. Inside the briefcase are the day's edition of *The Wall Street Journal*, several file folders marked "Brokerage Statements" and a checkbook, not the wallet style, but an executive two-ring binder holding pages of checks with perforated stubs.

Behind him, Mother's brow is wrinkled. I can almost hear her grousing, *Come on, Mike, keep going. You almost made me trip over you!*

Mother wears a babushka to protect her white curls from the wind, which most of us would refer to as a breeze. Her tapestry satchel contains an extra set of underwear, Dad's heart medicine, a stack of funeral prayer cards, spare batteries for her hearing aid, and garlic wrapped in a leftover bread bag: *There's no use leaving it behind in Florida, you'd just have to throw it away, and anyway you can always use garlic.* Not that I am privy to the contents of Mother's satchel, or Dad's brief-case for that matter, but some things a daughter just knows.

On this late May evening shortly after six o'clock, the sun is still shining and warm. Mother and Dad have come from their Deerfield Beach condominium to spend the summer in Lancaster, Pennsylvania, where my sister Pat and I have settled with our families. Our parents have visited us here before, but never for an entire summer.

"Just try it," I urged Dad at the end of their last visit. "It'll give you and Mother some relief from the intense Florida heat."

"We'll see," he said.

At the baggage claim, we find no navy canvas suitcase with its identifying red pompom attached to the handle, no collapsible metal luggage roller tied with rope inside a brown tote bag. Finally, the conveyor belt screeches to a halt, empty. Their luggage is lost. Not the best way to start a trip, but Dad will take care of it.

The vanilla-painted block wall is cool to my bare feet as I do handstands against it, counting aloud to see how long I can stay up. It is Pittsburgh in the late 1950s. The cellar kitchen of our sprawling rancher on Waldheim Road. I am six. My sister Patty, twelve.

"Get down before you crack your head open!" Mother snaps.

I was going to get down anyway. It stinks in here. Mother is giving Patty a Toni home permanent wave. Seated next to the mangler—a roller-based contraption into which Mother feeds sheets to press them—Patty hands her a small rectangle of tissue, then turns to look at me. Mother yanks a strand of my sister's hair.

"Oww!" Patty cries.

Mother smacks her. "Be still, I said!"

Patty's perm, a bit on the frizzy side, is fodder for our older sister's teasing.

"Hey, Chimunga!" Marge later taunts, as she lifts a plate from the sudsy dishwater. Patty dries, and my job, as the youngest, is to put the dishes away, a cycle of responsibilities that shifts each time a sister marries and moves away. Lena, twenty-four and already the mother of three young boys, is doing her own dishes in her own kitchen across town, with KDKA radio blasting 1940s swing oldies as Lena hums along. Dee, also married, lives up the street with her husband and son. She is petite and stylish with a voice that shrieks like fingernails against a chalkboard whenever she spies smudges on the wall or crumbs left on the table. It is as if each smudge, every crumb imposes upon her the same tribulation as when our mother—umpteen years ago—forced Dee to carry a bushel basket of dirty laundry up and down the stairs twenty times to punish her for whining about her chores.

Now in the cellar kitchen Patty sasses Marge, who is seventeen.

"I'm not a Chimunga!"

"Are too."

"There's no such thing as a Chimunga," Patty argues. She swipes her dark brown frizz with the back of her hand, then grabs another dish from the drainer.

"Oh, yes there is!"

"Then what is it?"

Marge wipes a bubble from her chin with her shoulder, then throws back her head, laughing, as if the word really does have a meaning, as if its meaning is even too atrocious to reveal.

"It's not even a word," Patty says.

"Is too, Chimunga." Marge is relentless. "Ask Daddy." Our father is the authority. The final word.

"Daddy!" Patty yells up the stairs.

"Get those dishes done!" Mother hollers back. Even though Mother is deaf in her left ear, the result of Ménière's disease, there is no escaping the echoes bouncing off the tile cellar floor and cement block walls. "And lower that radio!"

Tonight the Crosley is tuned into music—the same radio that delivers the voice of the Pittsburgh Pirates, Bob Prince. "Kiss it goodbye!" bellows Prince, to which our father always echoes, "Kiss it goodbye!" as if it takes both of them to confirm that, indeed, their team has scored a homer.

Marge picks up a dishtowel, spins it into a twist, and takes a swipe at Patty's backside. "Chimunga! Chimunga!" Since Marge brings me Twinkies each Saturday after working the checkout at Kroger's and forces her boyfriends to let me win at Uncle Wiggly, I don't doubt a word she says. Soon all three of us, armed with dishtowels, are swiping at each other, squealing, until the sandpapery voice of Arthur Godfrey beckons from the Crosley radio.

Oh, I don't want her, you can have her, she's too fat for me … he sings. We drop the dishtowels and hurry to our positions, me standing on Marge's feet and holding on around her waist, Patty and Marge locking arms. The three of us lean to one side, stepping into the polka as the music bounces off the walls.

This is the room where we eat dinner most evenings, pasta every Thursday, fish on Fridays, our mother's Italian cooking. On Sundays we eat in the sterile white kitchen upstairs, but here in the cellar we gather around the yellow laminate table.

"Bless us, oh Lord, and these thy gifts …" Our father recites the blessing, as the rest of us bow our heads and make the sign of the cross. Then we dig in, pasta first, meatballs and salad next. If we're lucky, there are Mother's artichokes

stuffed with breadcrumbs, parmesan cheese and garlic, sop-
ping with olive oil. From each leaf, our teeth yank a deli-
cious combination of artichoke meat and stuffing, as we aim
for the prize at the bottom: the tender, delectable heart.

Usually one of my sisters mentions our cousin's momen-
tous artichoke-eating blunder: the time she ate the prickly
needle-like lining of the heart. Dad points toward the white
porcelain stove across the room or the laundry tub next to
the sink.

"Look over there!" he exclaims. His voice is so full of
excitement, it is impossible not to do as he says. Time and
again, one of us turns back to her plate to find the coveted
heart missing. And there at the head of the table is our father,
swallowing, then laughing.

"Daddyyyyyy!"

Here in the cellar kitchen, Mother does our laundry, the
washer and dryer lined up against the wall next to the mangler. Here we pile onto the glider with cousins and nephews,
swinging until the glider smacks the painted block wall and
Mother yells at us to stop. Here a steady stream of uncles,
aunts, cousins, sisters, brothers-in-law, and nephews arrive at
the bottom of the stairs. Sometimes they come at Dad's invitation for a feast prepared by Mother and served at tables
pushed together in the adjoining game room. At other times
they head for Dad's office next to the kitchen, the hub of his
construction business and the place where family problems
are discussed. At the time, I know nothing of this cousin's
crisis or that cousin's trouble in school, but I do know that
occasionally his six brothers turn to my father when they
need a level head and an extra dose of common sense to
help think things through. It only takes a phone call for Dad
to offer, "Come over to the house. We'll work it out." Afterwards, as our relatives troop back up the cellar stairs, there is
an air of relief about them.

As Arthur Godfrey sings the "Too Fat Polka," Marge and Patty and I move as one to the rhythm. Underneath mine, Marge's feet are sure, and she sings aloud with Arthur Godfrey.

Oh, I don't want her, you can have her, she's too fat for me ...

Patty chimes in, *She's too fat, much too fat*—her footwork equally accomplished. Floating atop Marge's feet, embraced by my sisters, I feel safe. We are without a hint of the loss awaiting us years from now, three sisters clustered together two-stepping across the brown and cream checkered floor.

The doctor's waiting room is decorated in shades of blue and gray with artificial trees that don't need watering and never die. A picture window offers a view of hectic Route 30, giving the impression that patients are seated on the safer side of the window. Prior to his arrival in Lancaster, Dad phoned me to ask that I find him a hematologist here. He had just started a regimen of weekly Procrit injections, he explained, because his hemoglobin count had been dropping, rendering him highly anemic.

It is Friday, the day after their arrival. Dad's car is en route, scheduled to arrive from Fort Lauderdale via a car transport company in five to seven days, so I've driven Dad to the doctor's office in my car. This will also give me a chance to show Dad the route between the hematologist's office and Valleybrook, the apartment complex where I found them a two-bedroom summer rental. Other than the few days until their lease commences, Dad wouldn't think of taking up residence in the guest room of either Pat's home or mine.

"After three days, fish and visitors stink," he asserts. Dad's paraphrase of Ben Franklin's adage cuts the eloquence, but makes the point.

Now the nurse calls Dad's name. He follows her to the scale. A recent issue of *Guideposts* sits on the table beside me, its masthead dubbing it "The magazine for successful living," which compels me to pick it up. The first article is written by a Cuban, ambivalent about leaving behind his homeland to make a new home in America.

This is the year of Elian, the six-year-old Cuban boy who was plucked from the ocean after the boat in which he and his mother and stepfather sailed from Cuba had capsized. Both adults drowned, leaving Elian to brave the waters until rescued by an American boatman. A political and court battle ensued to determine if Elian should be kept by relatives in America or returned to his Cuban father. He was eventually returned, taken by force from the home of his Miami relatives, but not without a fight pitting family against freedom. It is an arguable choice. The heartbeat of hearth and home, the familiar voice and smell and touch of one's papa. Or the opportunity for freedom, to choose a path and follow one's dream. It seems unconscionable to be deprived of one for the sake of the other.

My father's voice startles me.

"Jan!" At the nurses' station, he is motioning for me to accompany him.

"Sometimes two sets of ears are better than one," the nurse asserts.

Not my set, I think. Medical jargon is like computer technology, as far as I am concerned: indecipherable. And why an extra set of ears? Just for Dad to schedule weekly injections? Isn't it obvious—from his very demeanor—how utterly capable Dad is of running his own life? I rise and go anyway.

In the examining room, Dad and I sit side by side waiting for the doctor. When I was a child, it was Dad who accompanied *me* to medical appointments. Mother never learned to drive, so whenever my sisters and I had to go somewhere—

music lessons, school activities, dental appointments—it was Dad who drove us there.

"There's nothing to worry about." Dad's advice in the doctor's office was always the same. "Nothing at all. Just keep your mind on something else. That mountain out the window over there—beautiful, isn't it?"

Finally Dr. McClenahan would enter the examining room. One time, I remember, he peered into a mysterious wooden box filled with bottles and jars.

"Hmm, kindergarten vaccination," he said. "Let's see, I have Bugs Bunny and Mickey Mouse here. Which would you prefer?"

"Do you have Annie Oakley?" I asked.

Dr. McClenahan and Dad exchanged smiles.

"By golly, I just might," he said, then rummaged through the box. "Yes, here it is, right here. Annie Oakley."

I looked out the window as Dad had suggested, but the mountain was blurry and the pain piercing.

"See? Nothing to it," Dad asserted. "Nothing to it at all."

Not wanting to disappoint Dad, I bit my lip and held back the tears.

Now Dad is the patient, and my role here is questionable. Dad has always been a private man, fiercely independent, and though he seems at ease, his poker face could win an Oscar. I feel like an intruder.

The clock on the wall is inching toward noon. His appointment was at eleven.

We chat about family. The upcoming reunion we've planned for the Fourth of July weekend. Though the reunion typically includes just our immediate family, Dad says he is thinking of also inviting his youngest brother and his wife, my Uncle Johnny and Aunt Marie. Sounds great to me; I love those two.

"Maybe we should hire some entertainment," Dad suggests.

"Entertainment?"

"For after dinner on Saturday night."

"What kind of entertainment?"

"Like a comedian or some kind of music. So people don't eat then just feel like it's time to go home."

"I know of a magician. Well, he moonlights as a magician. He's actually an optometrist."

"Yeah, something like that," Dad says. "Why don't you look into it?"

"It's probably going to be expensive."

"Whatever it is. I'll pay the bill. See what you can come up with."

We catch up on news about relatives. Stories about Dad's golf buddies in Florida. How they kid around on the course. How they all went to Naples for a weekend golf outing and it was only $248 for the whole package, everything included. How one of them is being sued by his stepchildren for the money his late wife left him.

Where is this doctor? It feels awkward knowing that, if I were the one being seen, Dad would be out in the hallway, rounding up the nurse, asking what's taking so long.

"I want to ask the doctor about something called myelo-dysplasia," Dad says. "The doctor in Florida mentioned this in connection with the anemia, then we got to talking about something else, and I didn't get a chance to ask him what that was."

Finally, there is a knock at the door.

The doctor is forty-ish with wavy brown hair. He could pass for a Brooks Brothers model in his pressed navy pants and blue button-down collar shirt. He apologizes for the wait, shakes Dad's hand, then shakes mine.

"Visiting from Deerfield Beach?" he asks Dad.

"Yes, I'm up here to spend the summer with my daughters."

The doctor scribbles something on a yellow Post-it Note and attaches it to Dad's file. He says he has a friend, Brad somebody, who lives and practices medicine in West Palm Beach. Maybe when he goes to visit Brad, he'll stop by and visit Dad. It seems odd for him to make such a comment when he has known my father for less than a minute. He glances at the medical file. There appears to be a mistake.

"How old are you?" he asks.

"I'll be eighty-seven in November," Dad says.

"Really?" He writes the number down on another Post-it Note and attaches it to the records, another oddity as Dad just provided this information on the form he completed. "You look like you're in your sixties!"

This is true. Dad's skin is supple and tanned, his dark eyes are bright. But now he is finished with the niceties and ready to get down to business.

"Doctor?" he asks. "This myelodysplasia I have—what is it?"

The doctor hesitates. Then he says, "I believe in telling the truth."

"Of course," Dad asserts.

"I mean, I prefer being straightforward with patients."

"Well, certainly!" Dad's voice reveals his impatience, reflecting my feelings as well.

"Well, myelodysplasia is a rather new term," he explains. "The name for it used to be pre-leukemia."

On the doctor's tie, a pattern of brown dogs reminds me of Katherine's stuffed toy named Bones. The dogs seem to move along as if on an escalator. As a child, I had a recurring nightmare of riding on escalators, unable to get off. I would awaken in the night trying to shake the image of zigzagging lines moving me into oblivion.

The doctor's eyes rest on mine.

"It's not genetic," he offers, his voice attempting to soothe. How could he! I feel like grabbing him by the tie and strangling him! But, of course, I sit quietly through his description of the various blood cells and their functions, the stages of the disease: myelodysplasia, myelodysplasia with blasts, myelodysplasia with extreme blasts, and, finally, acute leukemia. His scholarly tone nauseates me.

It is suffocating in here. There are blank spots in my listening. Blank spots interrupted by the face of Carl Croft, the boy who sat alphabetically in order behind me in seventh grade homeroom. Coco, then Croft. I didn't know Carl very well. He was a lanky boy with deeply tanned skin and a jet-black crew cut. One day Carl was absent, and our homeroom teacher told us that he had leukemia. I didn't know what that meant at the time. I just knew that Carl never came back.

Now the doctor hesitates; he repeats that he believes in telling the truth. If he says this one more time, I swear I will slap him. He says older patients cannot sustain the treatments offered to younger patients. In younger patients, it could take four to six years to advance to acute leukemia. In patients who are Dad's age, it might take up to a year.

"Has this all been explained to you before?"

"No," Dad answers. He is sitting beside me. Without looking at his face, I can feel his somberness.

Leukemia? *Leukemia?* It was always Dad's *heart* that threatened to slow him down. After a quadruple bypass, the surgeon told him he could possibly look forward to another eight to ten years of life. That was twenty-four years ago. I remember him, home from the hospital, unbuttoning his shirt to display the scar, his voice revving up as he described the procedure of cutting the breastbone with an electric saw.

Then, half a dozen years ago, his arteries were clogged again. This one ninety percent. That one ninety-nine. Another eighty-nine percent. His condition rendered the golf course off limits. It prohibited his daily hike around the reservoir, restricted him from lifting a grandchild onto his knee. In spite of Dad's repeated requests, the doctors refused to chance a second bypass surgery. The risks were too great, they insisted. His age. The scar tissue still unhealed from the first bypass.

"Life is for the living," Dad asserted. "I can't just sit around all day twiddling my thumbs." He decided to roll the dice. All or nothing.

My brother-in-law phoned from Pittsburgh, concerned.

"Damn, he's stubborn," he said. "He's gone from one cardiovascular surgeon to the next until he found one willing to perform the surgery."

And again, Dad outlived the doctor's prognosis. Oh, it's lurked in the shadows, but Dad's incessant focus on the future can be enticing. That, at least, is part of it.

I am usually the last to get a joke, the quickest to lose my way on a road trip, the clueless one. But when it comes to Dad's mortality, it's not been for lack of grasping that I've disregarded it. Much of it, I know, has been a pushing away, a refusal to entertain—even well into adulthood—the notion of earth without my father here to anchor down the edges.

But now the facts, spoken with authority, jar me. It is a powerless feeling to sit here without the insights to challenge the doctor to rethink this. I remember a day eight years ago when my best friend uttered words that made her impending death seem undeniable. It was a Sunday in July, sweltering hot, and we sat cross-legged, facing each other from opposite ends of her sofa as she broke the news that the cancer was spreading.

"The x-rays looked as if someone took a handful of sand and threw it up in the air," Elaine said. She was still dressed in her church clothes, a sheer dress with a pattern of autumn flowers. She wore a curled brown wig to hide the effects of chemotherapy.

"You know, I keep wondering *why*," she said. "I'm thinking maybe there's something God's trying to tell me." Her voice was raspy like a woman of seventy, though she was only forty-three. She enumerated the possible messages God might be trying to convey; it made my heart ache to hear her ponder them. Did she work too much? Did they live too extravagantly?

"I do work hard, but I've never neglected my family," she concluded. An understatement for a woman who baked from scratch and sewed her own curtains. "And we do live comfortably, but we don't live beyond our means.

"Then I was reading the Bible," she continued, "and I saw discrepancies in the teachings of the Catholic Church, and I thought, 'That's it! That's what God's trying to tell me: I'm in the wrong religion!' The coronation of saints—it's not even in the Bible, you know?"

She seemed to be on a faraway island, in a place of which I had no knowledge, but I nodded in agreement simply because I loved her, and I didn't want her to waste her breath—of which there was very little—explaining something I probably wouldn't understand anyway.

So Elaine was on a mission to find a new church. She and her husband had celebrated with the Lutherans, the Methodists, and today they'd visited St. Thomas Episcopal.

"This is the one," she said. "This is the church where I belong."

Elaine didn't live long enough to return to St. Thomas. The next Saturday, shortly after her parents had arrived from Johnstown, she curled up on her bed and died. It is devastating to lose a friend. And since God, more than anyone, knows this, it was with Elaine's words about St. Thomas, *This is the church where I belong*, that he used my dearest friend to lead me to the place where I would be drawn to his son.

But suddenly I am afraid again. My fists are tight at my sides, the way I often felt before I knew Jesus, a relationship so new that I've barely explored the boundaries of it. Am I supposed to turn this over to God? *Totally*? If he has a plan, I need to know what it is. Perhaps like Elaine, I should search for a message. No, a roadmap. It feels as if I need to *do* something, take charge somehow. Suddenly it seems that having faith and actually *surrendering* to that faith are two separate matters.

The doctor's voice startles me. "If you'd like, I can pump up the dosage of Procrit," he says. "You're at 30,000 milligrams. We can try 40,000. Maybe alleviate some of that tiredness?"

"Whatever you say," Dad concedes.

The doctor scribbles on another Post-it Note, sticks it on Dad's chart. The silence presses in on us. "I'll call my nurse, so you can meet her," he offers. "The one who will administer your weekly shots."

The nurse is a chirpy brunette who smiles, but not without empathy.

"We're going to pump up the Procrit by 10,000 milligrams," he advises her. "Hopefully alleviate some of Mr. Coco's tiredness."

The nurse gives Dad the thumbs-up sign. I would rather haul garbage than have her job.

As we exit through the front door, Dad makes a feeble attempt at sounding nonchalant.

"Well," he says. "He didn't tell me anything I didn't already know. Nobody lives forever."

Over lunch at Lapp's Restaurant, it is hard to know what to say.

"When we pray for you, what do you want us to pray for?"

"No suffering," he says.

At first, we don't tell Mother. Through the years we've come to negotiate the truth for something less in exchange for a semblance of well-being. So that she can understand Dad's tiredness, we tell Mother he is anemic and leave it at that. This attempt to shelter is not a family trait of which I am proud. It is simply one that is.

Mother moseys through our garden with my husband.

"What are those called?" she asks. "Over there."

"Those are Joy Sedums," Randy says. "They turn ruby red in autumn."

"Is that a weed?" Mother asks.

"No, that's going to be a Shasta daisy. Bright yellow."

The two of them stroll in the warmth of the late spring sun. Randy points out the buds on the rosebush, the purple wisteria starting to bloom. Mother shares with Randy the ingredients to her homemade *bracciole*; he asks how much of this or that she puts in, how long she cooks it. Though Mother is nearly deaf and can barely hear most of us, she always seems to hear my husband's voice.

"I think it's because he's so patient with her," I tell Dad. "He doesn't make her nervous about not being able to hear. Unlike the rest of us who get edgy when she keeps saying 'What?'"

"You're probably right," Dad admits.

Dad turns his thoughts toward the delayed arrival of his car. He is on the phone once, sometimes twice a day to the transport company. Each time he calls, he gets a conflicting report on the car's whereabouts. First, they claim it's at the Florida–Georgia border waiting for another pickup. The next time, he learns that it has not yet left the terminal in Fort Lauderdale.

One operator chastises Dad for calling too often. Another asserts that his car can't be transported until there is a shipment of at least three or four cars to make. He asks when exactly they expect to have that many cars, and the operator gives him the verbal equivalent of a shrug. One reminds him that the five-to-seven day delivery time is merely an estimate, not a guarantee, per the fine print in the contract. Typically, Dad is quick to rebuke less-than-satisfactory service. In this case, however, he strives to maintain harmony with the operators.

"The problem is that they have my car *and* their payment." He shakes his head. "That's why you should never pay before receiving service. *Never.*" He keeps copious notes of his telephone conversations, writes down operators' names, calls them back at precisely the time they say they might have more information. They never do.

On Thursday, June 1, Mother and Dad move from our guest room into their summer apartment at Valleybrook. They have a suitcase of clothing—the one that was lost but retrieved—that they brought on the plane with them. The rest of their luggage is in the trunk of the Cadillac somewhere en route.

"Why don't you stay at my house until the car arrives?" I offer. "That way you can just use *my* car when you need it."

But the time limit for fish and visitors has passed. We stock their refrigerator and kitchen cabinets with groceries. In boxes, I have packed family photographs, quilts, sheets, pillow shams, toss pillows, and other accessories to make their furnished apartment seem like home. The boxes, groceries, and two lounge chairs for the balcony fit in the back of Randy's SUV, which I borrow for the day. It is awkward to carry all these things to the second floor unit, but it is important to do so without my parents' help. The anemia has rendered Dad's energy at an all-time low, and Mother has had colon problems, a mastectomy, and her right hand is weak from arthritis.

"You two just stay here in the apartment." A preposterous suggestion. As futile as trying to contain toddlers to the living room while all the fun is outside. They carry groceries. They hoist boxes. They climb the stairs red-faced and breathless, then walk the long pathway back to the parking lot to get more.

"Sit down!" I insist.

They both play deaf.

Later I tell Randy about the escapade. He raises his eyebrows.

"You couldn't have waited until Saturday, when I could have helped with the moving?"

The next morning, their front door is unlocked, so I let myself in. I am here to drive Dad to pick up a rental car.

"Hello?"

No answer.

At the top of the stairs and across the hallway, Mother is puttering in the kitchen. Dad doesn't appear to be here. He's not in the master bedroom. Not in the spare bedroom. Not in the bathroom. Not in the living or dining room. Mother still hasn't noticed me. She is deaf in her left ear and in her right wears a hearing aid that is nearly useless. To keep from scaring her, I stand back from the kitchen door.

"Hi, Mum!"

She doesn't hear. I yell louder.

"Mother, hello!"

Still louder.

"Mother!"

She turns and faces me.

"Where's Daddy?"

"He walked to the store," she says. "I needed oregano."

"He *walked*?"

"I'm making sauce. I'll put some in the freezer, what little room there is in that freezer. She had parsley here in the cupboard." The landlord uses this unit for her own vacations; part of the deal of renting it was that some of her belongings would remain in cupboards and closets with the kind invitation for my parents to use anything they wished. "My oregano and *basilico* I packed in the suitcase that's in the car. I can manage without the *basilico*."

The store is a mile roundtrip, a brisk walk for anyone in *good* health. It is already eighty degrees outside, however, and Dad's hemoglobin count is plummeting.

"I have to go get him. It's too far to walk."

"Oh, he'll be okay." She swats the air to dismiss my concern, then opens the freezer door. "See how I moved all her junk over to one side?"

"When did he leave?"

"What?"

"When did Daddy leave?"

"About forty-five minutes ago. Maybe an hour. Here, look. The stuff on this side belongs to that lady. And I'm putting all my stuff over here."

The inside of my car is stuffy, the heat oppressive. I gun the engine and crank the air-conditioning knob. This is just like him not to wait. Going to extremes not to inconvenience. It would have taken me one minute to stop at a store!

A block from the apartment, there he is about to climb a grassy knoll, panting, sweating. In one hand is a grocery bag. In the other, a folded copy of *The Wall Street Journal*. I punch the window button and lean my head out.

"Dad, what are you doing? It's eighty degrees out here! That's too far to walk!"

He shrugs, lumbers around to the passenger side and gets in. His breathing is heavy.

Deep inside, he is still the curly-haired four-year-old—more than eighty years ago—who rode the neighbor's dog like a bronco in front of his parents' Windber, Pennsylvania, house and store. It happened right after a funeral procession had departed from the nearby Catholic church. Whenever he told the story, he was right there watching a horse-drawn buggy carrying the casket up the narrow road, followed by more buggies carrying mourners. On the roadside, old Italian women in black wailed and waved hankies, their flags of death, crying *Se benedicte amate*. The details of the day came alive through his telling.

After the procession had passed, my father spied the German Shepherd at the edge of their property. He snuck up on the dog and petted it. With both hands, he held onto its back and jumped, then jumped again—as high as he could—until he finally mounted it. The dog took off, and he grabbed hold of its fur and held on tight as the dog galloped across the gravel. Together they dove under the front porch, wooden slats scraping my father's head. That was his earliest memory, riding the dog. The memory that, it is said, reveals character.

"Did you fall?" I asked, as he recalled it, laughing the whole way through.

He nodded, still laughing. From the twinkle in his eye, I could see that it was the ride, not the fall, that hailed vivid in his mind.

A week goes by, then another. And another. Still no car. Dad's patience is wearing as thin as his blood. It is as if he is grasping for some measure of control. He will expose the transport company, he decides, to keep others from being duped. After he gets his car, he will contact an investigative reporter at the Fort Lauderdale *Sun Sentinel*. Or he'll call Pat's daughter, Suzanne, a journalist for the *Stuart News*. He'll share his story; he has it all documented. He'll be glad to let them use his name.

Finally, after four weeks and a letter written by an attorney, the car arrives. There is a small bit of damage, a scratch or two. He is out the $525 he paid for the transport service, several more hundred dollars in a rental car, a few hundred more in attorney's fees. A third of his summer vacation is behind him without having had the convenience of his car. He is eager to share this plight, as if it is the uppermost thing on his mind. Though he says nothing of the blood cells failing to perform their role in his aching body—not a mention of his illness—he reveals every detail of the car transport company's failure to deliver his car.

After the car is here, we hear nothing more of the planned exposé. His focus shifts to a plan to return his car home to Florida by summer's end. Perhaps he will hire another transport service into whose reliability he carefully checks. Or maybe one of his great grandsons, on college break, can drive the car south, then fly back. But each attempt to solidify plans for the car's return is foiled. Even with guarantees and references, Dad is wary of transport companies. The drive, we convince him, would require too much energy to handle on his own. And the timing may not work out for his great grandson to help. It seems as if the car is not meant to make the trip.

Two

Crossing the
Highland Park Bridge

Fir trees—they must be a hundred years old—tower high above the two-story building across from my parents' Valleybrook balcony. In a shaded spot under one of the trees, a tin pan filled with bread scraps attracts a company of squirrels, birds, and rabbits, as if nearby, instead of a 1970s apartment complex, there might stand a charming cottage in the woods. One squirrel seems to take charge; Mother has nicknamed him "The Boss." The Boss only need arrive for the feast, and the other animals make way. The woman who lives in the ground-level unit shaded by the firs, according to Mother, fills the pie plate and nearby water bowl daily.

The wildlife provides ongoing entertainment for Mother and Dad. Birds zoom in for a landing, then carry away dinner takeout style. Rabbits twitch their noses, watchful for the other animals' exit before sidling up to the supper table. The squirrels seem to stomp their feet and snap imaginary suspenders, nodding for the others to busy themselves elsewhere.

"Look!" Dad's voice is full of wonder. "Over there! Watch

how that bunny rabbit goes for the dish as soon as the squirrel takes off!"

This is the same man who used to hunt rabbits during
small game season, then during deer season take up his rifle
and head for the Alleghenies. He would don a red-and-black
plaid wool jacket with a hunting license in a clear plastic
pouch pinned to the back, pull on black waterproof boots.
He and his brothers and their buddies would be gone for
days, returning full of boisterous laughter and stories. Once,
Dad hid in tree branches above the freshly fallen snow. When
his youngest brother arrived below scouting for deer, Dad
jumped from the tree to his shoulders, setting Uncle Johnny
in motion like a Mexican jumping bean. Dad could hardly
contain his laughter each time he repeated the story.

One year upon their return home, Uncle Carmel, my
father's oldest brother, taunted me with the story that Daddy
had shot Rudolph up there in the mountains.

"He did not!"

"Here," Uncle Carmel said. "Go take out the garbage.
When you come back, I'll tell you about it."

Our garbage cans sat in a notch of pavement at the top
of our driveway. As I approached them in the darkness, a
large stiff form came into view, sprawled across the top of
the two cans. At first I couldn't decipher the shape, but suddenly there it was: a thick side of fur, a rack of antlers. My
arms loosened around the Kroger's bag, and it crashed to
the driveway as I turned and ran toward the house, my heart
thundering.

"Was that really Rudolph?" I asked Dad later that night.

"No," he assured me.

Still, there was something scary about the image of that
carcass, knowing my father was responsible, then later seeing the stuffed head of a buck mounted to our game room

wall. One minute Dad's power would unearth me, the next I didn't see how any child could live without it.

Each New Year's Day, for instance, Dad guided my sisters and cousins and me on hikes that seemed to take us halfway around the world. Bundled in boots, mittens, and hats, we set out for destinations such as the Pittsburgh Zoo, the Carnegie Museum, or our Aunt Helen and Uncle Paul's house on Mount Royal Boulevard. Each trip was a thrill, not only because of what we found when we arrived, but because we had overcome the obstacles to get there. Seven miles. Ten miles. Snow. Below-zero temperatures. Numb fingers. Freezing toes. Dad led us across the Highland Park Bridge singing "I've Been Working on the Railroad," telling jokes to distract us from the brisk weather, pointing out the wonders of nature to subdue our complaints of aching feet.

One time someone mentioned that some people drink booze to keep warm. As if on cue, my father piped up.

"You know, I've never touched a drop of liquor in my life," he said. "Never even wanted to. And I'll tell you why."

He took us back to the 1920s, to the attic bedroom of 4606 Liberty Avenue in Pittsburgh, his family's home above the Liberty Avenue Fruit Market, owned and operated by his parents. The bedroom, shared by my father and his six brothers, spanned the length of the three rooms below it, their beds wedged in dormitory-style.

"My parents took in a penniless uncle," Dad told us. "He showed up from Italy with nothing but a steamer trunk. No job. No money. They let him share my brother Carmel's bed, which sat perpendicular to mine.

"Right away this uncle won my affection. He was always doing magic tricks. Or singing and dancing. Or telling stories from the old country. I just loved him.

"My relatives tried to dig up work for him—construction or some kind of maintenance job—but he couldn't hold down a job because he had a drinking problem. He'd get paid, send a little money to his wife and kids in Italy, and spend the rest on liquor. He was supposed to be saving money to bring his wife and kids here from Italy, but that never happened.

"I remember after everything quieted down at night, I'd pretend to be asleep but peek out the corner of my eye. There'd be a sliver of light from the moon. It was just a matter of time until I'd hear my brother's bed squeak, then the steamer trunk scrape against the wooden floor as my uncle slid it from underneath the bed. He'd unlatch the lid, then pull out a paper bag with a bottle inside. Sitting on the edge of the bed, my uncle would tip the bag to his mouth and gulp and gulp and gulp.

"He lost everything he had," my father remembered, sad now. "All because of liquor. That made quite an impression on me. I vowed never to touch the stuff."

"What ever happened to him?" we wanted to know.

"Oh, he ended up moving from one relative's house to another until he died. Never saw his wife and kids again."

Sometimes my father used his stories, like this one, as teaching tools. Sometimes to entertain. And other times they were simply precious heirlooms lovingly passed from one generation to the next.

In the streetcar on the way home, it was warm snuggled next to him. He instructed us to close our eyes and picture a kitten yawning, and when we did, all our mouths stretched wide in yawns. "The power of suggestion!" he said, so full of laughter that it was impossible not to laugh with him.

Now here we are on a journey without an inkling of the path ahead of us. Can we trust God, the way we trusted our father to lead the way? Shouldn't we simply surrender the path to the one who knows the way, the one who can comfort and lead us through the pain? We should. But I think of the desperate man in the Gospel of Mark who exclaimed, "I do believe; help me overcome my unbelief."

As much as I hungered for my father's approval, basked in his encouragement, there were times, especially as a teenager living under his rule, when I found him barely approachable. "The Boss" in living color. This was the case whenever a boy asked me for a date. To accept, of course, Dad's permission was imperative, the most dreaded fact of my teenage life.

"No." His most frequent answer.

"Why not?" Even as I asked, his stern expression unnerved me.

"I said no." There was no further discussion, no revelation of my father's thinking on the matter. He would simply peer back at his newspaper page, and I would walk away devising a plan to meet the boy on the sly.

Mother was quick to acquiesce to Dad's judgment. Still she had her ways of getting what she needed, which often involved one of us.

"Tell Daddy you made the chicken," she would say. "He doesn't like chicken, but if he thinks you made it, he'll say it's good."

When Lena and Dee, my two oldest sisters, were young, Mother insisted they stay dressed in their church clothes long into Sunday afternoon.

"Stand on the front porch," she would order them. "If Daddy sees you all dressed up, he might say 'Let's take a ride.'"

Brought up on a farm by impoverished Italian immigrants, Mother's limited education, intensified by poor hearing, made her insecure in the face of our father's accomplishments. When she could, she'd delegate to one of her daughters the awkward role into which she was thrust.

"Here." Mother pushed a pen, then a small, plastic-covered box of thank-you notes toward me. "Write something. For the tea set they gave us." She wrung her hands. She knew this would happen if he won the election. It was 1967. Stacked on our kitchen counter were leftover Kiwanis Club posters for the Pennsylvania district governor campaign. On them was my father's portrait and the winning slogan: "GoGo with Coco."

Now she would have to entertain. As the district governor's wife, she would have to follow him to meetings across the state, wear cocktail dresses, sit at the head table and make conversation, write thank-you notes each time the local clubs presented them with gifts. Her handwriting, as scraggly as a seven-year old's attempt at cursive, embarrassed her.

"It doesn't look nice," she asserted.

"So what?" I offered. "Some *doctors* write like that, too."

"Just write," she said. "It's pewter. I hope you know how to spell 'pewter.'"

I was sixteen years old. I knew how to spell. I was tempted to refuse, not for lack of empathy, but because her surly demands always triggered insolence in me. Instead, I picked up the pen.

"Go ahead, write it."

She must have felt like a tourist in a strange land as she tried to keep pace with my father, an accomplished entrepreneur who was afraid of nothing. Their worlds were so different. When forced to navigate my father's terrain, my mother was lost, anxious to retreat to the safety of her kitchen, the world she had mastered.

It was Dad who planned our vacations, Dad who signed report cards, Dad who arranged our music lessons, Dad who drove us to friends' homes. He never raised a hand to any of his five daughters, barely even raised his voice, but we dreaded disappointing him. There was nothing worse than being called downstairs to his office for "a talk." He would lecture us from across his gray steel desk, a spiel that often began with a statement of his disappointment.

"You know how I feel about smoking," he once said to me. Earlier that day he had come looking for me at the Midas Touch Beauty Salon and saw me smoking under the hairdryer, then he turned and walked out without my knowing he was there. I was sixteen years old at the time. "Was it one of your sisters who influenced you?"

"No," I said. Though every single one of my four sisters did smoke at the time, it didn't seem accurate or fair to incriminate them.

I don't remember the details of his lecture, but I can still feel the tan leather of his office sofa sticking to the backs of my legs, the tears burning behind my eyes.

For as long as we did smoke, even well into adulthood, my sisters and I tried to conceal this fact from our father as if we were sixth graders hiding in the girls' room. We'd be on vacation at the shore—all of us married with our own families—and the sound of our father's approaching footsteps precipitated a panicked shoving of ashtrays into a drawer or the flushing of cigarettes down the closest toilet. There was no denying the smokey haze as he entered the room, but Dad was wise enough to know that, as adults, his daughters would make their own choices. We knew that he knew. And he knew that we knew that he knew, and it was simply left at that.

He took every opportunity to encourage our success, and there was nothing as motivating as his approval. A successful school project. A performance of the school band. Dad was never reticent about expressing his pride in us. "I knew you could do it," he would say. "Wasn't a doubt in my mind." Or, "You know, I have always enjoyed the traditional Christmas carols, especially sung as expertly as your choral group just did." Or, "Fantastic putt! You're a natural golfer!"

Now, suddenly, we are confronted with the limits to Dad's power, limits that we believed did not exist. They sneak up from behind like sucker punches. Dad goes about living, trying in earnest to make the best of things, then suddenly the swift blow, the loss of breath, a sharp pain in his side, another decline in the hemoglobin count, the relentless fatigue.

A spongy ball flies through the air at Neffsville Park. Six of us—ranging in age from seven to eighty-six—stand in a large circle, Velcro racquets in hand. The ball flies toward Dad. He swings his racquet under his leg, catches the ball and waves, half-smiling. Soon after, he sits on a nearby bench and drops his racquet next to him. It is impossible not to notice that an entire day's worth of energy was poured into his effort not to spoil anyone's fun.

At nearby Mount Gretna Lake, Katherine swims out to a wooden platform in the middle of the lake for her first jump off a high diving board. Dad watches from the dock, his forehead wrinkling with concern as she swims farther and farther out. He slips off his shoes and socks, as if readying himself for the rescue. What is he thinking? If Katherine *would* happen to get hurt, then what? If he heard his granddaughter screaming for help, saw her going under for the third time, how would a grandfather reconcile the fact of his physical inability to swim out and save her?

Another visit to Mount Gretna. Dad loves the wooded paths here, the Adirondack chairs sitting out in front of summer cottages whose porches are strung with twinkling white lights. We wander into the Jigger Shoppe—Dad and Mother, Katherine, her friend, and I—for homemade ice cream, Dad's treat. For years now, because of his heart problems, Dad has resisted the temptation of his favorite dessert, settling instead for frozen yogurt, which is kinder to the arteries. This evening, however, he orders a chocolate fudge cone, the real thing. Certainly there's a change in perspective when time is short, but the changes in Dad's choices still take me by surprise. Surprise filled with sadness.

The tables have been cleared after dinner at Betty Groff's Farm Restaurant where we have come to kick off our family reunion weekend. We are gathered at two long tables of ten in a private dining room, where we feasted on Betty's famous Chicken Stoltzfus, ham, prime rib, buttered noodles, mashed potatoes, corn, chow chow, homemade bread, apple butter, cracker pudding, chocolate cake, ice cream, and shoofly pie. The magician has finished his performance in front of the corner fireplace. We are still trying to figure out how he could have produced the eight of hearts, the exact card that my nephew Peter's wife, Marissa, selected only in her mind. Uncle Johnny returns from the kitchen where he has slipped off to pay the bill.

"No!" Dad insists. "This is my treat."

"Too late," says Uncle Johnny, triumphant. He has an agile build, though more solid than when he was younger. "It's already paid for."

"Why should *you* pay?"

Generosity is a trait shared by Dad and his brothers. Having just arrived from Pittsburgh this afternoon, Uncle Johnny has yet to learn of his older brother's illness. Dad's face hardens as he slips his wallet back into his pocket. Footing the bill is one of the few indulgences still under his control.

Earlier today Dad awaited his youngest brother's arrival like a kid on Christmas Eve. He skipped his usual nap and delayed eating lunch in the off chance that Uncle John and Aunt Marie would arrive with hearty appetites.

On Sunday, family and food and laughter warm my home. My father is telling stories on the screened porch. He dishes them out as freely as Mother heaps pasta onto our plates, always more where that came from. He has repeated his stories so often that we can recite them by heart. Still we love to listen and to watch the expressions on the faces of those new to our gathering—a recently married spouse, a new boyfriend or girlfriend.

"My father, as you know, was a very, very strict disciplinarian," he says of our Sicilian grandfather. Dad's eyes light up as he returns to his boyhood when he and his older brother were dueling in their parents' store, "just playing around the way kids do," as he describes it.

"Pop had gone upstairs to dress to go to the hospital," he begins. "Our ten-month-old sister had just died from pneumonia there. We didn't have a phone in those days, but one of our neighbors did, and they came to get Pop for the call. He came back in and went upstairs without a word to us, so we didn't know what was going on."

Dad doesn't remember who started it: His brother Carmel picked up a butcher knife and Dad grabbed the sharpener, a long, pointed poker. Each held one hand behind his back and off they went, backwards then forward, two miniature swordsmen dueling past shelves of canned peas and corn, down the aisle of toilet paper. They taunted and dared each other.

Come on, come on. Touché!

They shimmied around the front counter, ducking down and popping up on opposite sides. From his post, Dad faced the door that connected the store to their home upstairs.

"When my father opened the door, " Dad says, "I caught a glimpse of him. We didn't dare act up in front of him. I immediately dropped my dagger and snuck away to hide upstairs under the bed."

His brother, however, was unaware of their Pop's presence. From behind the counter, Carmel jumped with a flourish and a loud *Touché!* And as he did, into his head gashed the shiny sharp edge of a meat cleaver wielded by their grief-stricken Pop.

The wound in his brother's head. The blood pouring into the bathroom sink as my father helped wash it. Their Pop's anguish at the loss of a second child, his firstborn having tripped as a toddler into a vat of boiling laundry water. None of these are the point of Dad's story. There is a slight bravado in his telling of it. He relishes his reputation for coming out on top, savors the memories that illustrate it. Even until Uncle Carmel died at age eighty, Dad razzed him about the escapades in which he outsmarted him. Uncle Carmel always laughed, too, poking fun at himself for bearing the brunt of his younger brother's antics.

But now Dad's edge is diminishing. It is the final event of our weekend-long family reunion. We are again gathered around tables, this time on a covered outdoor terrace at Bent Creek Country Club. It is the annual Fourth of July picnic.

"Come on, John." Dad pushes away from the table and motions to his brother. "Let's take a walk."

Buffet tables spread with hamburgers, hot dogs, barbecued chicken, corn on the cob, and Caesar salad snake their way through the outdoor cafe. An hour goes by, then another. The chairs next to Mother and Aunt Marie remain empty. I try not to imagine their conversation, try not to hear Dad's matter-of-fact voice repeating the doctor's prognosis to his youngest brother, try not to picture the forlorn look on Uncle Johnny's face.

Crowds of picnickers hold drinks and chat, or lounge on blankets around the practice tees. Kids with their faces painted wander through the crowd, cats and clowns and princesses, some with stars or flowers on their cheeks, licking pink cotton candy or slurping sno-cones. In the Moon Bounce, they knock willy-nilly into each other, laughing with delight as they spring from the billowy surface. A disc jockey's music blasts from the balcony. Katherine requests "Celebration," my sister Marge's favorite song, and before long the song lyrics blare from the speakers, "Celebration now, come on!"

"This is for you, Aunt *Margaret*!" Katherine emphasizes my sister's full first name, which no one except our mother calls her.

Marge holds her iced tea in the air as her sandals tap the pavement, her silver hoop earrings jiggling in rhythm with her side step. The rest of our family step back, pretending not to know her.

In a nearby sand trap, a giant sand turtle hails proud, the creation of Katherine and two of her cousins. The turtle has garnered first place honors in the sandcastle contest. Our family's cheering section gathers nearby on a grassy knoll as I snap open my camera's lens cover.

The camera frames a photo in which the sun is setting. Short ones in front, tall ones behind. Kneeling in front of her smiling family, Katherine holds a flag with the winning sand castle entry number, six. In the distance, the white clubhouse looms. Somewhere inside, Dad and Uncle Johnny sit in what appears to be a business meeting chaired by my father. He is solemn yet professional as he tenders his notice to end his consulting service to the construction company he founded and built with his brothers. Soon the night sky will explode with fireworks—scarlet, emerald, sapphire, magenta—cascading like Niagara Falls, bold and mighty, then swirling to the ground, their glowing embers put to rest.

The first time my father told me that he loved me, I was thirty-five years old. It was a declaration that convinced me he was going to die. Never had I doubted Dad's love, but until that moment he had never expressed it in words. They were spoken over the telephone one evening right before we hung up. Out of nowhere.

"I love you, Honey."

The kitchen stool on which I sat suddenly felt wobbly. *Something must be terribly wrong!* I thought. *No!* I wanted to say. *You can't say that! Not after all these years! It doesn't count!* For nights afterward I couldn't sleep, certain that Dad had been given a death sentence of which the rest of us were unaware. *It must be his heart again,* I decided. *Something with which he doesn't want to burden us.* It has always been a paradox in our family: the effort to avert each other's grief by hiding the truth, planting the even deeper agony of suspecting and not knowing.

Finally, I called my friend Howard.

"My father is going to die," I told him. "I'm sure of it."

It was midafternoon on a weekday, and the other tables at the Swamp Fox were empty. "I cannot imagine being on earth without my father. I'm scared. It will feel as if the ground has disappeared from under me. As if I'm standing on air. As if I have no roots."

On that afternoon in the dimness of the Swamp Fox, a picture of my father emerged, like a photograph lifted from its processing chemicals. The man who brought orphans home—Marcella, Ruth and Mary—from a Pittsburgh orphanage to share holidays with his own family. The man who drove four hours, and would have driven forty, to help his daughter paint the woodwork in the two-room office of her new advertising business. The man who would sometimes cause his daughters to dig in their heels against the intensity of his caring, unable to stop protecting, stop helping, stop loving.

On my lap a mound of crumpled tissues grew until my sobs were quelled by the comfort of Howard's listening. Finally, he spoke.

"You have to tell your father everything you just told me," he said.

Tell him? It was an unfathomable idea. How could I express such emotion when all my life the love between us had gone unspoken?

"I cannot imagine my daughter feeling this way about me and telling a complete stranger instead of telling me," Howard insisted. "I would want to know."

The following Christmas, the sun bounced off the hardened snow outside the renovated marshmallow factory where the offices of my advertising agency were located. It shone through the ceiling-high windows, warming the brick walls and dancing on the teal carpet. Dad and I had driven here from my Walnut Street row home where Mother and Dad were visiting for the holiday. With Dad sitting across from me at my desk, I began to read a letter I had written, his Christmas gift. The paper fluttered in my hands, jittery and cold; the typewritten words began to blur.

This was hard to do. It felt schmaltzy—all this reminiscing—but genuine and tender at the same time. In the letter, I reminded Dad of a telegram he'd sent me, yellowed now, but still tucked among my treasures. It was dated February 13, 1965, my freshman year in high school, and sent to me at my oldest sister Lena's house where I was staying while he and Mother were vacationing in Florida. It said, "Mother and I are thrilled that you made the W-T honor roll. But not surprised. We knew that you could do it. Love, Dad." Now, more than twenty years later, I thanked him for his encouragement.

I reminded him of the ten-dollar bill he once gave me so that I could pitch in for the gift my friends and I were planning to give the cabdriver who drove us to school each morning. When, for some reason, we decided not to buy the present, I returned the money to my father. Dad expressed appreciation for my honesty in returning the money to him; he pointed out that not all kids would have done the same. Today, in another place and another decade, I thanked him for this gift to me, the gift of integrity.

In the letter, I described the pride on his and mother's faces, two candles lit in a darkened crowd, as I walked down the steps of Old West to receive my college degree. It is a powerful revelation when a child realizes that she would have been nowhere without her parents' love and support, yet there they are giving her all the credit.

It was the intangibles for which I thanked my father, the offers of encouragement and hope and values. My promise to him was to pass those same gifts—the ones he had given me—on to my own daughter. We hugged that day in my office, tears streaming down my face. Dad cleared his throat and said a parent could not receive a finer gift. Years later, after he was gone, I would empty the contents of his desk drawers and find photocopies that he had made of the letter. And then in his dresser drawers, more photocopies of the same letter.

Someone once said that nature is God's first missionary. Certainly it is how God manifests his presence to my father. Autumn after autumn when I was a child, a procession of family cars, Dad's car out front, headed to Port Allegheny for a weekend in the mountains. I can still feel the car braking to a halt, still hear Dad admiring the painted leaves or the deer positioned at woods' edge. "A masterpiece," he would say. He knew just where to find mountain springs and urged us to cup our hands and take a drink.

"It doesn't get more refreshing than this," he would say. "Here, drink all you want. You can't buy water this fresh."

Dad and his brothers led us on hikes along mountain paths—sometimes seven or eight miles long—dozens of us, while singing, telling jokes, searching for walking sticks to help negotiate steep hills. On the mountaintops, we rested on fallen logs.

"Timber!" yelled our cousin as he leaned against a dead tree and it toppled to the ground.

"Timber!" yelled another cousin, then another and another and another, dead trees falling everywhere.

Uncle Johnny scooted ahead and hid behind a hill of rocks, waiting to be approached by a threesome of aunts. As they walked by, Uncle Johnny leaned out from the rocks.

"Where ya' goin', ladies?" he chided, making our aunts scream and jump, and eliciting peals of laughter from the uncles and cousins.

When we arrived at a prearranged spot, there would be more aunts and more uncles, their cars backed into the clearing, with homemade sausages and peppers, hamburgers, and hot dogs sizzling on camp stoves. There were fresh Italian rolls, dozens of donuts, cookies, coffee, hot chocolate. Here we shared hiking stories and posed for photos. One of my favorites, a photo of Mother and Dad, was shot when they were in their mid-forties, not much younger than my age now. In it, they are standing beside Dad's 1959 Cadillac convertible. Dad, with his flannel shirt collar open exposing his undershirt, is stretching his left arm back to rest his hand on the hood of the car, and his other arm is around Mother's shoulder. She is wearing pedal pushers and a white blouse with rolled up sleeves, and the way they are laughing, I can just hear one of my uncles cracking a joke as the shutter clicked.

On a trip before I was born, an uncle had charge of my sister Dee and her girlfriend as they hiked through the woods. Engrossed in conversation with another adult, my uncle neglected to keep track of the girls and suddenly realized they were missing. This was in the same mountains where another relative once mistook Dad's beloved beagle for a rabbit, cocked his hunting rifle, and shot him. Dad arrived at Brownie's side to find the dog crippled and writhing in pain. Heartbroken, he loosened his grip on his own rifle.

"Just finish him off," Dad muttered and then walked away.

Now my father was outraged at his brother-in-law's carelessness. Those who knew the woods set off on various paths calling the girls' names. They searched for hours and, as darkness crept over the mountains, their hearts grew heavy. Finally, making their way on barely lit paths, Dee and her friend emerged from the forest to shouts of relief.

Many years later, Dad and the rest of us lost Dee forever. I will never forget my father's faltering voice long distance over the telephone; my second-to-oldest sister had died. Forty-nine years old. Heart complications, sugar diabetes. It was November 6, 1984, the day of President Reagan's reelection.

"Who are you going to vote for?" Dad had asked at her hospital bedside, adamantly focused on her future.

"Me," she whispered with one of the last breaths she took.

Eight years later my parents lost another daughter, their oldest, Lena. Just before she died, Lena had been the life of a family cruise we'd taken to the Caribbean. I was eight months pregnant with Katherine at the time. My sister was eager to experience each activity listed on the daily schedule that every morning was slipped under our cabin doors. In spite of what she thought was a chest cold, she danced and laughed and swam and shopped, calling the rest of us party poopers when we begged for a break. Three months later, she was gone. Lung cancer. Dad was stone faced. It was like a three-act play with all the scenes performed out of order.

During both of my sisters' illnesses, Dad remained steadfast in search of their cure. He pored through medical books, contacting well known doctors, top medical facilities, leading research hospitals. Stacks of photocopied articles grew ever higher in my parents' living room. Exhausted from it all, Dee at one time said, "If he tells me to go see one more doctor, I swear I'm going to scream!" It was as if Dad believed that he himself would find the cure for diabetes and, later, for cancer. When it came to his daughters' well-being, it seemed there was no obstacle too enormous for him to conquer. After they were gone, my father never relinquished his positive spirit but, knowing Dad, my sisters' deaths had to have been the most excruciating defeat he ever suffered.

Now that Dad's fatigue is increasing and his hemoglobin continues to drop, I am desperate to help him. Somewhat like Dad's, my own sense of responsibility tends to err on the side of excess. It's like a trick Satan plays on me—*If you really care, then you'll do something about it. Ask God for direction? Naaa, that could take too long. Get going; figure something out!* This invariably stirs up commotion, a free ticket for Satan to the matinée. As far back as I know, people in my family have been sliding into the driver's seat.

As a boy, Dad watched his beloved grandfather fill the role of doctor, even though he was not educated as one. Nonno had brought a medical book with him to this country from Sicily. The book, Dad recalls, was six inches thick, filled with names and illustrations of herbs. It catalogued the medicinal value of each. With the shortage of doctors in the early part of the twentieth century, many of their Windber, Pennsylvania, neighbors looked to Nonno and his book to cure their aches and illnesses, even to set broken bones.

Dad remembers Nonno as a robust man who always wore a charcoal-colored woolen cap, indoors and out. At an early age, my father and his brothers were expected to greet their grandparents the first thing upon rising each morning.

They lined up in Nonna's and Nonno's two-room house behind their own to kiss the back of their grandfather's hand, then repeat the gesture with their grandmother.

"*Se benedicte amate*," they said. Bless you, Grandfather.

The blessing over, the fun began.

Nonno sat on a wooden rocker in the bedroom, taunting and teasing. My father dashed past him, and Nonno reached out as if to grab him. My father, in telling the story, is right there, his voice laced with excitement. He is taking in Nonno's laughter, feeling his own boyish squeals rise from the heart, the door slam as he runs out the back of the house, only to turn around, sneak back in through the side door, and risk being caught again and again.

"He was well respected," my father asserts. His brown eyes sparkle, reflecting the memory of his grandfather, as if in a mirror. "Well respected and all fun."

Dad recounts the gloomy day he accompanied his Pop and Uncle Sam to dig up Nonno's remains from the cemetery two miles from the church in Windber. They gathered with the undertaker at Nonno's gravesite while a hearse waited nearby to carry the casket to Pittsburgh. It had been decided that Nonno would be reburied next to his wife, Nonna, who had moved to Pittsburgh with Dad's family shortly after her husband's death, and recently passed away herself. From Nonno's grave, the undertaker heaved one shovel of dirt, then another. I do not know what my father was thinking while he waited there, but I imagine he pictured the Nonno he remembered, the robust man in the gray woolen cap who played with him as a little boy, the jovial man for whom his love deepened through the years.

"So we were standing there while the undertaker was digging, and he got down to where the casket box was, and there was no longer a casket." Dad's voice is solemn now. "There had been dampness there, and even the box—they used a wooden box back then—was rotted and gone. And all there was was a skeleton, just the bones and a few ... "

My father pauses, and I see that he is right there, a young teen standing at his grandfather's grave. The sadness on his face is almost too much to bear. His words are spoken slowly, quietly, as if he has to squeeze them from his heart, as if he has forgotten the tape recorder I have placed on the table to capture the stories of his past.

"It looked like straw hair from the scalp. You know, the scalp was there, but there was no flesh of any kind, just bones. So the undertaker was there, of course, with the hearse, and he brought up what was there ..."

As he says this, my father's eyes are moist with tears. His voice trails off, unable to continue. His hands rest powerless in his lap.

Positive Thinking

My first meaningful dose of religion came in the third grade. This was when I made a deal with God. It was at the end of the school year, my sights set toward fourth grade and which teacher we'd choose if we could. For me, there was no question. Miss Hiller was captivating with her gentle smile, her softly curled dark hair, her blue eyes gazing through black-framed glasses on each child as if he were her own. She was tall with graceful hands and, besides being pretty, she'd traveled to Japan; word was that she even taught her students to speak Japanese. After suffering through a year of Mrs. Burger, who sat behind her desk munching Wise potato chips and snapping reprimands at Barbara Ahl for no apparent reason, Miss Hiller beckoned like Glinda the Good Witch of the North.

"Please, God." My hands were folded in prayer. "Give me Miss Hiller for my fourth grade teacher. If you do, I promise I'll write you a poem."

The first day of fourth grade came, and there was my name on the class list posted on Miss Hiller's door. I wrote the poem in God's honor, the first I'd ever attempted, and no doubt God nodded, having planted the seed for a passion that he knew would take root and grow.

As an eight-year-old, especially a Catholic eight-year-old, I was perplexed by religion. For one thing, why did I go to school with the "publics" when I was Catholic? I could never figure this out and was sure, especially when the Sunday school nuns directed us public school students to church pews separate from the Catholic school kids, that we were sinners, every last one of us, for schooling with "the publics." Secretly, however, I was glad that, whatever their reasons, my parents had chosen to spare me from the nuns on a full-time basis.

St. Scholastica was a modern church in the 1950s, minimalist in comparison with the more ornate Sacred Heart in East Liberty, for example. There were no intricately carved statues, no dark mahogany pews, no painted angels hovering overhead on arched ceilings. Instead, St. Scholastica's statues were simple cement-gray figures, the pews a light-colored wood, the lines angular, not curved. Even the stained glass windows were downplayed, long rectangular slivers with only a subtle splash of pastel color. It was as if the neighbors in our well-to-do Fox Chapel suburb didn't want to appear *too* Catholic; but with names like Garrity, Fitzgerald, and McCrea, they may as well have worn their scapulars on the outside of their Brooks Brothers shirts. Our family marched a third of the way down the aisle each Sunday, paused, genuflected, and entered our customary pew on the right side of the church.

On the kneeler alongside my parents and older sister Patty, I searched my soul for the presence of sin, large or small. My soul appeared to my young imagination as the living room of a house, furnished with a sofa, two armchairs, a coffee table, a couple of end tables, a floor lamp, and various accessories. It was the tidiness of this room, its cleanliness, which was to be scrutinized. If there were chairs askew, afghans slung willy-nilly, cushions sloppy on the sofa, lampshades tilted to the sides, I knew my soul was soiled with sin, certainly not fit to receive the body and blood of Christ at communion. The power of guilt, a double whammy from an upbringing that was both Italian *and* Catholic, taunted me. But if the living room was orderly, I took it as a signal of permission to step right up to the altar.

Religion in our household was a private matter. Though we were forced to have it—as in go to mass every Sunday and holy day, attend catechism classes, and bow our heads in grace before dinner—we never discussed it. Perhaps there was a Bible in our home, though I don't remember seeing anyone read it. Every Sunday after mass, my father sat in a wing chair in front of our living room picture window, peering through black-framed glasses at the *Sunday Roto* and studying the words of his idol, Dr. Norman Vincent Peale. I'd tiptoe past Dad, trying to escape a second Sunday sermon, but this was a man who could spot the movement of deer miles away in the woods. Soon I was held captive to the powers of positive thinking, courtesy of Dr. Peale and my father who incessantly quoted him.

"You can do anything you set your mind to, Janice." Typically, this was how Dad wrapped up our little sessions. "Mind over matter, remember that. Mind over matter."

My mother, tiny and gray-haired, embraced the rituals of Catholicism. In church, her fingers skittered across rosary beads as though she were endlessly crocheting. In the early morning hours, she sat at our yellow laminate kitchen table, holy cards protected by Saran Wrap fanned out in front of her like a Royal Flush, reciting prayers for the dead. She didn't impose these rituals on us except for one: We were not to enter the church without first covering our hair. If one of us forgot to bring a lace mantilla, we were forced to wear a tissue atop our dark brown hair. Why God took this as a sign of respect—our walking into his house wearing the very item into which people blow their noses—I could never fathom. But the topic was not open for discussion; we simply did as our mother said.

After Sunday mass, we public school kids attended catechism classes in the Catholic school adjacent to the church, where we sat on wooden seats connected to the school desk behind. In fact, we sat on just half of the wooden seat, in obedience to the nuns who instructed us to reserve the other half for our guardian angels. The nuns dimmed the lights for slide presentations, whose only feature I retained was the sound of the accompanying record player's *ding* alerting the nun to proceed to the next slide. Most of the time I spent imagining my guardian angel who, at first, looked remarkably like me—dark brown hair, dark brown eyes—until I changed her to a tall blonde with blue eyes. Then, like a protective mother, I began worrying whether my guardian angel had enough room on the seat beside me, whether she was hungry. When I could, I would sneak M&Ms into the Sunday school classroom and slip them inside the desk where I sat. The following week, the M&Ms would be gone, which made *me* feel angelic to have provided my heavenly connection with nourishment. No one ever mentioned the M&M's, and this confirmed all the more that they were a secret between my guardian angel and me.

The nuns told us stories of children whose evil parents or guardians refused to take them to Sunday mass and how the children trudged through snow and ice storms, sometimes for miles, to arrive at church on their own. The stories made me long for the opportunity to establish my own godliness. They filled me with the hope that my own parents would cross their arms and deny me the privilege of church so that I could defy them and also be praised by the nuns. In my imagination, the warmth of grace rushed through me as I reached the church door, disheveled and out of breath, genuflecting, making the sign of the cross.

As teenagers, forced by our parents to attend Monday night CCD classes, we sat in classrooms under fluorescent lights while the lay teacher, usually a volunteer, droned on through the students' cracking of their gum, boys ribbing and elbowing one another, spit balls flying across the aisles. Finally, I convinced my father that spending Monday evenings studying Ancient History and Algebra II would be of greater value than this weekly festival of clowns.

In college, Sunday night mass was celebrated in the basement of Old West. Students sat cross-legged on the floor, a welcome informality. But the sermons were weighted by irrelevance, and soon I opted for chatting with friends in the dorm or heading to the Milton for a hotchee-dog.

During my married, divorced, married-again years, I was an on-again, off-again churchgoer, there sometimes because it felt good, sometimes out of a sense of obligation. I've always believed in God, though later a spiritual advisor would remind me that even Satan believes there's a God! Randy and I married at St. James, an Episcopal Church, because having both been married before, the Catholic Church was not an option. The open arms of the Episcopalians appealed to me, and since Randy didn't care one way or another, we stayed at St. James.

Soon after my friend Elaine died, her words about St. Thomas Episcopal Church came back to me. "This is the church where I belong." Curious, I decided to visit. When I walked through the front door, it seemed as if Elaine herself were there. As if she had just put on a pot of tea and we were settling in at her kitchen table for a long chat. The sermons, given by a priest who in a former career had practiced labor and criminal law in New York City, enticed me. He described scenes from movies to illustrate his points. He admitted his own shortcomings. He was real. The people of St. Thomas treated Randy and me as if we were family stopping by for supper. Nothing fussy. Just pull up a chair, stay as long as you like. It felt comfortable.

For several years of Sundays we sat in the pews taking it all in. We had Katherine baptized at St. Thomas. We were there when one pastor departed, when another served an interim term, and then when Father Bill joined us from a church in California. During the transition at church, I was going through a transition of my own: selling the business I had founded seventeen years before, now hoping to spend more time writing and with family. I joined a group at church called Mothers of Preschoolers and later, when Katherine started Sunday school, I sat in on a parent discussion group. My involvement was minimal, but it was the most I'd ever participated in a church.

Then Randy and I signed up for a course called Alpha. Randy took Alpha, he said at first, because he figured I wanted him to. Later he admitted that he was on the fence about this Christianity business and he wanted to get off of it one way or another. I took it because my understanding of Christianity felt vague, and Alpha billed itself as a course in basic Christianity. In spite of my church attendance all these years, I wasn't clear on who Jesus was. The father–son relationship of God and Jesus confused me. Why did people use the two names interchangeably?

At first I was suspicious of the program, half expecting

people to cross their arms and raise an eyebrow whenever I asked a question. While I was becoming enamored of this guy who gave up his life and died on a cross for me—the God who had come to earth as a human, I discovered—I was looking out of my other eye trying to figure out what these people wanted from me. There had to be a hitch. I'd been in the advertising business much too long to think otherwise. Was I being brainwashed? But why? Other than a free will offering basket on the buffet dinner table, they never asked for money. And for what devious purpose would they encourage a personal relationship with the most moral being who ever lived?

My deepened faith in God, and the various forms in which he manifests himself—Father, Son, and Holy Spirit—didn't arrive in a thunderbolt of a moment. It was more like a feeling that crept up on me. I would be driving along Route 222 and there, to my left, a patchwork quilt of farmland and trees that I'd driven past hundreds of times before would suddenly take my breath away. The beauty of its workmanship struck me as amazing, a level of perfection that would have been impossible for any human to mastermind. Rows of trees a hundred feet tall with luscious greenery spilling into each other, fields planted in stripes this way and zigzags the other way, butting up to more farmland with equally impressive patterns. Only one being, someone with the big picture, could have envisioned the effect of the whole. Suddenly I was filled with an overwhelming sense of joy. My heart was so light it seemed to be flying. I couldn't wait to get back to Alpha. I couldn't wait to see my small group and share my discovery with them.

Other things started changing, too. Thoughts—different from any I'd ever had—unfolded in my mind, taking me by surprise. Once as I stepped out of the house to place a letter in our mailbox, the mail truck was just departing from our

cul-de-sac. Since I wanted to mail my letter promptly, I ran
after the truck. It stopped in the middle of the street, and
the mailman leaned out his window. His dark frizzy hair was
pulled back into a ponytail. He had a moustache. As I ran
toward him with my letter, he was smiling. A genuine, warm
smile. *My God, what if the mailman is Jesus? How would I know?
What if Jesus came back as a mailman?* I walked back into the
house, picked up my iced tea from the kitchen counter, took
a sip.

Then we were at a Saturday evening mass with my parents while visiting them in Deerfield Beach. There were
seven of us: Dad, Mother, Uncle Johnny, Aunt Marie, Randy,
Katherine, and I. In the pew behind us, about two-thirds of
the way down, a woman was crying. Sobbing actually. She
had come into the church shortly before mass began and
stood near the altar, apparently searching for someone. Finally, the lector announced the woman's name and said she
was looking for her husband. Behind us, her husband identi-
fied himself and when the woman joined him, they bickered
for a short time. And then she began to cry. Occasionally, her
husband would order her to keep quiet, but most of the time
he ignored her.

Her crying continued through the opening prayers,
through the readings, through the homily. The people
around her squirmed; their uneasiness was palpable, as was
the annoyance of my father, who does not embrace displays
of emotion. The pain I felt for the woman deepened until
I was ready to explode. Then, as if stepping out of my body,
as if forgetting my inherent shyness, I knelt on the pew and
crawled partway down it, behind my husband, behind my
daughter, behind my uncle and aunt, until I arrived at the
spot where the woman sat in the pew behind us. I reached
over, touched her, and she leaned toward me.

The smell of liquor engulfed her. Strands of blond hair had come loose from her French twist. Her eyes were red and swollen. I had no plan of what to say to her, but somehow the words were there.

"I don't know who you are," I whispered. "But I know that God loves you." And as the words came from my mouth, I knew that they were true.

"Oh, thank you!" she cried.

As we hugged I asked her name, and she told me.

"I will keep you in my prayers," I promised.

As Alpha progressed, Randy, who had been struggling over the chronology of dinosaurs, the Neanderthal man, and Adam and Eve, became intrigued by the Bible. The Bible! An unexpected addition to his Stephen King and Dean Koontz collection. Soon—and this surprised even him—he wasn't swearing at drivers who cut in front of him on the highway. He began answering "Excellent!" when people asked how he was. It was hard not to notice the change in him. With a nervous laugh, one of his friends asked, "This doesn't mean we have to stop drinking beer and golfing together, does it?" Randy himself admitted his relief at learning that Christianity didn't require wearing a tie or carrying a Bible so heavy that it could break your foot if it fell on it.

Our occasional weekday breakfasts out together at a nearby diner turned into a stream of questions and shared discoveries until one of us would look at the clock and say, "Can you believe we've been sitting here all this time talking about *God*?"

"Was there anything about the talk that especially struck you?" I asked. It was a brisk fall morning, my first attempt at leading an Alpha discussion group. Named the Ruth Group after the Old Testament woman whose story illustrated the beauty of a relationship in which the greatest bond was faith in God, it included eight women and two men.

The silence was thick, heavy. The ticking of my watch sounded thunderous. *God help me,* I prayed. *I have no idea how to do this.* The Alpha team training had assured us that the group leader's job was to facilitate discussion, not to answer questions and certainly not to preach. As the training had suggested, I silently started praying the Lord's Prayer, an effort to surrender the burden to God and free myself from it.

Finally, one woman spoke. Her voice was thoughtful, deliberate.

"Yes. I don't know if I believe in Jesus," she said. "I don't think I do."

"I don't think I do either," said another.

And with that, the Ruth Group was open to endless possibilities.

"I'm not sure I qualify for this," I said.

"For what?" Barrie asked. She was sitting across the table from me at Burger King. We had just finished an Alpha session. It was the first Alpha course being offered on Wednesday mornings at St. Thomas, and my friend Barrie and I were both, for the first time, group leaders.

"I'm not sure I qualify for being an Alpha group leader. I still have questions myself, you know."

"We all have questions." She scooped ketchup onto a French fry.

"Yeah, but mine are big ones."

"Like what?"

"Well, like the 'what about other religions?' question. It bothers me," I said. "I have friends who aren't Christians, really fine people, the best. They're compassionate and generous, always putting other people first. There's just no way I can believe they're not going to heaven."

I was expecting Barrie to say, *Yeah, but the Bible says the only way to God is through Christ.* But she didn't. In true Alpha style, she just listened.

"I mean, I believe for me it's true, that Christ is my ticket to heaven. That is my truth, the truth the way I understand it, the truth I accept. But isn't faith a gift from God? How can we insist that if other people don't believe, then they're out? I mean, isn't that judging? And isn't God the only true judge?"

Barrie kept listening. And I kept talking.

"There was this guy I knew. He said that his daughter was converting to Judaism and that he and his daughter had a fight about it. Finally his daughter said to him, 'So you think I'm going to hell because I'm not a Christian?' And you know what he said? He said, 'Yes, I believe you're going to hell.' Can you imagine hearing such a thing from your father? That killed me! Who are we to judge?"

"Well, that's true," Barrie said. "It's not up to us to judge."

"Someone in our Alpha group—a woman whose son had been dealt some cruel blows in life—asked Mildred about this very thing," I continued. "Mildred was our group leader at the time. This woman was really concerned. She said to Mildred, 'My son isn't a Christian. What does this mean?' And you know what Mildred said? She looked this woman straight in the eye and she said 'Your son is going to heaven.' She said, 'Your son is going to heaven because *you're* going to heaven, and God knows that heaven wouldn't be heaven for you unless he were there, too.'"

It would take a bit more growing in my faith before I would understand Mildred to mean that, even though we don't have it all figured out, God, the very embodiment of love and mercy and grace, does have it figured out, and his plan is far more glorious than anything we can possibly imagine.

"I just love Mildred," Barrie said.

"So do I."

"Is this for Catholics?" Mother thinks she is whispering to my older sister sitting next to her on the love seat, but the volume of her voice competes with Nicky Gumbel's British accent emanating from the television.

"It's for everyone," Pat assures her.

Nicky Gumbel, an Anglican barrister-turned-priest, is giving a talk entitled, "Who is Jesus?" This is the first session of Alpha recorded on videotape. Pat and I brought the tape to Valleybrook because we felt compelled to engage Dad in conversation about an afterlife, and this seemed like one of the least awkward ways to do it. Dad ignores Mother's interruptions, his eyebrows knit in concentration. Nicky summarizes the session with a quote from C. S. Lewis.

> *A man who was merely a man and said the sort of things Jesus said wouldn't be a great moral teacher. He'd either be a lunatic—on a level with a man who says he's a poached egg—or else he'd be the Devil of Hell. You must make your choice. Either this man was, and is, the Son of God; or else a madman or something worse ... but don't let us come up with some patronizing nonsense about His being a great human teacher. He hasn't left that open to us. He didn't intend to.*[1]

Sitting cross-legged on the living room floor, I am partly listening to Nicky's talk, which I've heard half a dozen times

before, and partly wondering how Dad is reacting to it. When
we were young, our parents took us to church every Sunday,
prohibited us from eating meat on Fridays, and ensured that
we made our First Holy Communion and Confirmation. At
home, however, nobody talked about God. The closest Dad
and I ever got to sharing feelings about our faith—though
in fact, it was merely a debate over religion—was later in
life, on an occasion when he and Mother were visiting from
Pittsburgh. We were sitting around the kitchen table in my
Lancaster condominium, when I announced my plans to
convert to the Episcopal faith.

"But Catholicism is part of your heritage!" Dad objected.

"I'm divorced, Dad. The Catholic Church won't perform,
or even acknowledge, my new marriage. Actually, once I re-
marry, I'm excommunicated."

"You just need to keep going to church. I know a lot of
divorcées who are still Catholic."

"But they won't give me communion. If I can't take communion, what's the point of going to church?"

"You can find a priest *somewhere* who will give you communion."

Mother typically stays out of such discussions. But now
at the table she was wringing her hands, fidgeting in her seat.
Finally, she could keep quiet no longer.

"The pope's the boss, Mike!" she said. "The pope's the
boss!"

Ignoring Mother, Dad continued citing examples of divorced couples, acquaintances of his, and their steadfast de-
votion to Catholicism. The debate continued, but my mind
was made up, and Dad's argument failed to sway me. When
he realized this, he ordered Mother to pack their bags and,
with nothing more to say, they returned to Pittsburgh. The
issue was never brought up again. Since then, Dad has vo-

cally championed unification among denominations, and I've taken this not as a sign of support, but at least as one of acceptance.

Now in the Valleybrook living room, my silent prayer is that Alpha won't open old wounds for Dad. Though nondenominational, the course originated at Holy Trinity Brompton, an Anglican church in London. If the course needs a sanction in Dad's eyes, perhaps that sanction is Pat, a devout Catholic, who has taken Alpha and who, like me, now serves on the Alpha team at St. Thomas.

Nicky bows his head in prayer. The session is over. My heart is thumping as I search for the stop button on the VCR.

"Well, what did you think?" I ask.

"A good talk." Dad nods, pensive. "He draws interesting analogies."

We ask Dad how he first learned about Jesus and he talks briefly about Sunday school when he was a boy. On three consecutive Tuesday nights we hold Alpha at Valleybrook. After Nicky's talks, our discussions are brief. Pat's time is limited because she is an early riser for work in the morning. Dad focuses on Nicky's delivery, affirms the accuracy of the message. Mother complains about deciphering the British accent; she is eager to discuss dinner menus.

The discussions fail to expose Dad's deepest thoughts. He seems to look forward to our Tuesday night sessions but, of course, he always welcomes the chance to spend time with his daughters. He appears interested in Nicky's talks, genuinely processing. But there is an awkwardness to our discussions afterwards. Talking about faith is a skill that our family has not mastered.

Why am I worrying about this? Certainly God—who has more love in his fingernail than all the rest of us possess together—has good plans for Dad. Perhaps my worry stems from my own stubborn blindness, my absolute cluelessness. All those years I called *myself* a Christian, this Jesus business was vague to me. Abstract at best. I certainly didn't know him on a first-name basis. It was more like "Mr. God," someone who might strike me down if I was having a bad day. There was a distance there. Now that I see Jesus as the gift God meant him to be—the ultimate expression of love—I feel different. Loved by a God who created a world in which people are free to doubt his very existence! Loved in a way that I can barely comprehend by a man who died that horrific death on the cross so that I can live, *really* live, in an unfathomable life after this one. It's a truth I cannot escape, a gift I must accept if I want to walk away with it—a life so incredibly perfect that it fires me with hope as I make my earthly pilgrimage toward it. It is impossible to want heaven so desperately for myself and not want it also for the people I love. But worrying is wrong. It's offensive to God who so exceeds my miniscule comprehension that it is ludicrous not to trust him completely. *Please, God, help me overcome my unbelief!*

It is a Thursday morning. The sunlight beams through my sunroom windows, casting angular shapes on the carpet. The Ruth Group gathers here every other Thursday, because when our Alpha course ended last Fall, saying goodbye was not an option.

We have just finished *A Life Worth Living*, a Bible study based on Philippians. We are discussing possible topics for our next study. One of our older members recalls a time, decades ago, when she heard a powerful sermon delivered by Dr. Norman Vincent Peale at a New York City cathedral.

"Well, why don't we study one of Norman Vincent Peale's

books?" suggests another. Her voice is articulate; she speaks in carefully weighed tones. "How about *The Power of Positive Thinking?*"

"Sounds good to me," says another, shrugging. "I could use some positive thinking."

The idea of studying *The Power of Positive Thinking* with the Ruth Group takes me off guard: the very topic that made me wince as a child, hoping to wriggle out of a second Sunday sermon! At the bookstore checkout, it seems inconceivable to be paying money for this book!

At age forty-nine, I am still that child when, for the first time, I open the book of my own volition. It makes me fidget and squirm, as if I'm standing before my father seated in the wing chair near our massive picture window. Outside, the azaleas are in full bloom, hot pink; the scent of freshly mowed grass is in the air. The sky is periwinkle and dotted with cottony clouds.

Slowly, miraculously, I am drawn into the pages. The Scripture quotes remind me of the peace that comes from relying on the strength of God, the concrete ways to stop worrying, to relax, to create one's own inner sanctuary in a fast-paced world. This is good stuff. I don't remember it this way. With each turn of the page, my childhood perspective slips further into the past, and a sensation of standing on solid ground fills me. My father's voice resonates from one chapter to the next: "Believe in Yourself," "A Peaceful Mind Generates Power," "How to Create Your Own Happiness," "I Don't Believe in Defeat."[2] I read and I read and I read, until finally the book rests closed on my lap.

F O U R

Long Term Capital Gains

D ad is nowhere in sight. He's not waiting at the edge
of the parking lot. He's not making his way down the
long Valleybrook sidewalk. It's not that we arranged for him
to meet me outside. It's just the way he does things, always a
step ahead, insistent upon not inconveniencing anyone.

The air is fuzzy, not quite a drizzle. It's Monday, July 31,
6:30 a.m. Not my favorite time of day, but Dad is usually
"up and at 'em" by five. At the apartment door, there is no
answer to my knock. Strange. Mother, of course, may still be
sleeping, or perhaps she hasn't put in her hearing aid. It's not
like Dad to forget a doctor's appointment. An orthopedic
physician, an acquaintance of Randy's and mine, squeezed
Dad into a hectic schedule for a 7:15 a.m. review of the
results of Dad's bone scan taken last Friday. In the meantime,
Dad's been on medication to alleviate back pain.

Again, I ring the bell, knock on the door, wait.

Nothing. My heart pounds. Something is wrong. Initially, Dad insisted on driving to my house so that I wouldn't have to wake up quite so early to accompany him to the doctor, but last night when I called and offered to pick *him* up, he didn't argue. This is not like him. Mother has whispered that he's been sleeping on the floor.

Finally there are footsteps. Slow, deliberate, the way a cripple might negotiate the stairs. When he opens the door, Dad's face is a putrid shade of olive. The corners of his mouth are turned down. He is straining to breathe.

"What's wrong?"

His eyes shift downward. "I'm a little short of breath." A *little!* "I've been awake since 12:30. Couldn't get comfortable."

"Do you have the medical records?"

"No. I couldn't make it over to where they were." He says this matter-of-factly as if the dining room table were located in Kansas. As if he didn't just play eighteen holes of golf a week-and-a-half ago.

"We don't need the records," I say. "Let's go."

The last time I saw him—last Thursday—Randy, Katherine, and I took Mother and Dad to see *Fiddler on the Roof* at a dinner theater. Dad's eyelids looked heavy, which he attributed to the back pain medication he'd started the day before. But he was captivated by the performance, called it "touching." Mother, it seemed, was the one who was suffering. She complained that the chicken was tough and then nudged me to follow her to the ladies' room. On the way back to the table, she said it was a good thing she didn't vomit on their rug. She fidgeted with the knob on her hearing aid, accusing Dad of buying her cheap batteries and chastising all of us for mumbling. The place was too loud, she said, too much noise, too many people talking.

"Would you like me to drive you home?" I offered.

"No!" she snapped. "I should have just stayed there in the first place."

As the lights dimmed and a hush fell over the audience, Randy rounded up a volume enhancer to boost Mother's hearing for the play.

"I don't want that thing!" she bristled, the sharpness of her words rising above the crowd.

Dad sat across the table from me in the darkness. The stage lights reflected in his eyes, tired but deep in concentration. Occasionally he joined in the singing—*Sunrise, Sunset*—as if no one else were in the theater but he and Tevye, commiserating about how quickly their little girls had grown into women.

Now as we leave Valleybrook, Dad's arm is tucked inside mine. The sidewalk to the car is a long, linear path, and all I can think is how unfair it is that Dad never had a son, a hefty brute of a guy who could get him to the parking lot without its seeming like an ordeal. Dad's 168 pounds lean on my 110 pounds, two inchworms bearing an impossible load. The old metallic red station wagon I'm driving—an embarrassing color attracting too much attention—is a loaner from the Volvo dealership where I've ordered a new car. In a corner of the windshield is plastered the model year '98 in orange neon numbers.

Finally inside the station wagon, my memory of how to get a car to move abandons me. It's not a stick shift. It's something easier. My mind is blank. I inhale, then slowly let the air around me settle. The key, first turn the key. The car starts, *thank you God*, and we pull out of the parking lot.

"At least we're going to the right place." I say this because, no matter how hard I try, I cannot think of another thing to say.

Dad stares blankly at the backwards neon '98 on the windshield.

"I stopped the medication," he explains between breaths. "For the back pain. The insert said if there's shortness of breath, stop taking it and call the doctor."

"So why didn't you call?"

"I didn't want to bother anybody," he says. "Not on a weekend."

"Please, we need to see the doctor as soon as possible." My father sits in a chair behind where I'm standing, his hands folded, head bowed. He does not go in for scenes, so I try to keep my voice calm, using my eyes to display urgency.

The receptionist barely acknowledges me. She glances around me at Dad, who appears to be resting, then she raises an eyebrow. This is clearly not the way she wants to start a Monday morning. I lower my voice to a whisper.

"Something is definitely wrong. My father could barely walk in here, he's so out of breath." It occurs to me to mention that the doctor is a friend of mine, but this woman does not look like the type who would be receptive to such information.

She rifles through a file for Dad's chart, pulls it out. She is in no particular hurry.

"How old is he?"

"Eighty-six."

Again she glances at my father, his supple skin, his smooth tan. For an eighty-six-year-old, even at his worst Dad looks about as bothered as his favorite singer, Perry Como. It is all I can do to keep from yelling, *Now! Get the doctor now!*

A woman who looks familiar to me is standing at the other end of the counter. Yes, I remember, I've seen her at the pool. She tells the nurse her appointment was supposed to be at noon, but that the doctor—a friend of hers, she mentions—told her to come in first thing, he'd squeeze her in earlier.

Oh, please, please take Dad first. But a nurse ushers the woman, who is slim and tan and healthy looking, back to an examining room.

Finally the nurse calls Dad's name. He stands and topples toward the side, grabbing the arm of the chair.

"Just a little light-headed," he says.

The nurse gets a wheelchair. A wheelchair! This reminds me of elementary school worksheets where the object in one column must be matched with the person in the other; and in our case, a terrible mistake has been made. My father in a wheelchair? But I follow the nurse's lead, and with our help, Dad sits in the chair. It appears that this nurse is going to leave us and go about her business. I throw her a pleading look. I don't have a clue how to operate this thing, wouldn't even know which lever to push.

In the examining room, where Dad and I wait, the silence presses in on us. The doctor's voice booms in the examining room next door; the walls must be made of paper. "So how's it going?" he asks the patient who looked like a cover model for *Fit & Healthy* magazine. They proceed to talk about a problem with the woman's hand. The doctor tells her about a similar problem that his wife once had. Inside I am screaming, *Come on! My dad could be dying in here!*

The doctor advises the woman to hold off on golf and tennis. They chat about golf and tennis. Dad is heaving now, his head bowed, as if it takes everything in him to dig deep enough for a breath. The woman asks about water skiing, what about water skiing, and the doctor says no, then explains in medical jargon why she shouldn't water ski. There is no question in my mind that if I were the one gasping for breath in a wheelchair, Dad would be raising a clamor in the hallway, *where the hell's that doctor?*

Finally the doctor strolls through the door. He announces that the bone scan was clear. By now, Dad's breathing problem has subsided, the way a car stops acting up the moment you arrive at the mechanic's shop. I mention it anyway, and the doctor takes a closer look.

"We need to get you to a *real* doctor," he jokes.

"I thought *you* were a real doctor," Dad quips back.

There's discussion about what kind of doctor he should call. A pulmonary specialist? An internist? Dad's family doctor? He has no family doctor in Lancaster; the only doctor he's seen here is the hematologist. We will call the hematologist.

My doctor friend didn't know Dad before their initial appointment the previous week, and I'm not sure if he realizes that, as good as Dad looks for his age, this is far from his usual condition. So, without exposing the depth of my anxiety, I tell him that. He stands to leave the room, and throws me a glare.

"I understand the urgency of the situation," he says through his teeth. "That's why I'm calling the hematologist."

Dr. Linley is a solid-looking man with round tortoise-shell glasses and kind eyes.

"I'm sorry you're not feeling well." He says this with such sincerity, I have to look again to make sure he is not a member of our family. It's a relief that Dad's regular hematologist—"the doctor of gloom and doom," as Dad calls him—has the day off. Dr. Linley asks about Dad's medications, listens to his heart, then gently removes the stethoscope from his ears.

"I'm afraid you're in heart failure." The pain medication, he says, sent Dad's hemoglobin on a nosedive, too much for the heart to bear. Then he looks at me.

"Can you drive him to the hospital, or shall we call an ambulance?"

"Whatever you think." There is a hollow space where my brain used to be; I cannot make a decision.

"You look as if you can drive him there." An indication, I suppose, that my skin is still in one piece; inside I am falling apart.

Route 30 is a maze of confusion; there is construction everywhere. Dirt that is dry from lack of rain swirls north, then turns south. Bulldozers make wrecking noises, spitting dust clouds that fog the exit signs. One sign appears to be printed by a child in orange letters against a black background: "Slow down. My daddy works here." Hundreds of times I have driven this way, but today the highway is exceptionally cluttered. There are chunks of cement from torn-down barricades, empty Coke cans from workers' lunches. Lancaster General is a hospital I know well, but I might as well be driving to Toledo; I cannot remember how to get there.

The Walnut Street exit looks familiar. As the car swerves off there, Dad steadies his hand on the dashboard beneath the neon '98. We drive across Walnut Street toward Lime, yes, yes, the hospital's rear entrance is on Lime. And Dad, his hand clutching the dashboard, has apparently been thinking about the meeting he scheduled with an investment manager arriving from Princeton this afternoon. My sister Marge, who is staying at my house, has driven here from New Jersey, and Pat will be taking the afternoon off, as Dad wanted the three of us to attend the meeting, as well. His face turning greener, he breaks the silence.

"Tell Tim Mountford to keep twenty-five to thirty thousand in long-term capital gains," he says.

Are you kidding? I'm thinking. *For heaven's sake, you're in heart failure!*

"Okay, Dad," I say. "I'll tell him."

We learn that Dad had a minor heart attack, a condition that has now been stabilized. A transfusion of two units of blood has raised his hemoglobin. But still there is back pain. An incessant ache in his lower left abdomen. There is dizziness. There is nausea. The specialists—cardiologists, urologists, hematologists—visit Dad in the intensive care unit, and of each one I ask the same questions.

"What's causing the back pain? The ache in the abdomen? The dizziness?"

And each time, they shrug.

"We can try an MRI," they offer, "to look for lesions on the vertebrae."

Or, "We can do a CAT scan. There may be something going on in the spleen."

Or, "Perhaps a urinalysis will show something."

But "the doctor of gloom and doom," back now from his day off, shakes his head. His hair is disheveled, his tie loosened. He speaks in hushed tones. On the other side of the curtain, the oxygen concentrator is whirring, the heart monitor beeping next to Dad's bed.

"They're not going to find anything," he tells me. "I *know* they're not."

He does not elaborate; I assume he means that these are simply symptoms of leukemia. And, of course, there is no cure.

"My father is hoping to return home to Florida," I say. "Is this going to be possible?"

"You people don't seem to understand! This disease is serious. He could *die* in three weeks!" Then he clears his throat. "Or up to a year."

A sensation not unlike drowning engulfs me. Why has no one taught me how to swim?

"So you think he should stay here?"

"Does he have relatives in Florida?"

"Not really."

"Then I think he should stay here," he says.

It is no use relaying his recommendation to Dad. From the beginning, my father has been put off by the "the doctor of gloom and doom," by his repeated recitation of the mechanics of cell deterioration, by his textbook delivery. Even at the mention of his name, Dad shakes his head and looks away. How can we convince Dad to stay here in Lancaster with us instead of returning to Florida to suffer alone? We will have to plead the case from our hearts. To start with, something must be done about Dad's dissatisfaction with his doctor.

"Dad, why don't you ask Dr. Linley to take over your case?" I suggest. "Next time he makes the rounds, why don't you tell him that you feel more comfortable under his care?"

Within twenty-four hours, Dad has a new hematologist.

"Bring me my checkbook." Dad's voice is raspy. He is propped up in bed, now in a private room on the cardiology floor. It is one of the rare moments when his dizziness has subsided, just as we are ready to leave for the evening. "It's a binder-style checkbook. In my briefcase in the bedroom closet. The key is on the ring on the dresser. The small key."

"Why, what are you going to do?" I joke. "Pay bills?"

"Just bring it to me. I want to look at it."

My sisters and I have spent the day wiping the sweat from Dad's brow as his temperature skyrocketed from a staph infection, consulting with doctors, eating in the cafeteria while Dad was sleeping. Mother has remained glued to a chair in the corner of his room, occasionally standing to check the level in the urination bottle and reporting on Dad's bathroom habits.

The next day, lying flat on his back, Dad writes checks in Marge's name, in Pat's name, and in my name. These are gifts to avoid as much estate tax as legally possible. The handwriting on the checks barely resembles his usual tidy script.

"See, this is why I'm Republican." He jerks his hand to dot an *i* and mutters something about "those damned Democrats." If he had the energy, he would launch into a tirade about the continuing mandate of estate taxes at the hands of the Democrats and the unscrupulousness of double taxation, referring to the president as *your* Clinton, a reminder of how it galls him that his own flesh and blood—all three of us—could have voted for anyone other than a Republican.

Even as he lies there in his hospital bed, weak and ailing, there is a tenacity about him, a fire that was set ablaze in childhood. A determination to endow his own family with comforts never found in the general store to which his parents were enslaved. Watching his mother and father work endlessly to feed and clothe ten children cut deep into his boyish heart, a wound that refused to heal. At five o'clock each morning, his mother began stocking shelves, and often she worked until eleven or twelve at night. His father, a bricklayer by day, donned an apron at night to restock shelves and sweep the aisles before closing. Throughout the night, my father and his brothers were responsible for guarding the produce on the sidewalk out front, taking turns ensuring that no one walked off with a watermelon or stole the cantaloupes. With eyelids drooping and one arm propped on a watermelon, he often fell asleep leaning against the brick wall of the store.

"It was always work, work, work. Sunup to sundown." Dad's lips tighten as he remembers. "My parents rarely took time to relax and enjoy themselves. I hated that store, hated how it ruled their lives."

My father's first taste of the independence for which he yearned came from a newspaper route and a construction job he held after school. Most of his earnings were contributed to the family's living expenses, but he stowed away the portion he was allowed to keep—nickels and dimes and quarters—in the rafters of the basement ceiling. At fourteen years of age, his savings in his pocket and a bag of personal items in hand, he boarded a bus for Cincinnati where he intended "to strike it rich." His plan was to rescue his parents from ever again having their work consume them.

When he arrived in Cincinnati, he rented a room for a couple of dollars a week. But finding a job was a different matter. By day he walked the streets looking for work, and by night, he returned to his room, dirty and hungry. It was from a letter he wrote to a friend back in Pittsburgh that his father discovered his whereabouts. One stifling Cincinnati evening, there was a knock at the door of his rented room. He opened the door, and there stood his father, a wiry Italian of few words but with a swift and powerful hand.

"Come on." His father only had to say the word; no one dared disobey him. Secretly, Dad was never so glad to see anyone in his life.

Now the four of us—Mother, Marge, Pat, and I—step into the hospital corridor. This has become the routine to give Dad privacy whenever he needs to relieve himself. It is time, we decide, to level with Mother regarding the seriousness of Dad's condition. So we tell her as gently as we can, unsure of how her nerves will withstand the worrying.

"I better take his dirty hankies back to the apartment." Her white vinyl purse dangles from her hand. "I can wash them and bring them back tomorrow."

It seems she's not hearing, not grasping the facts. We talk

a little louder, and without shouting, we try to tell her again. *Dad is terminally ill.*

"I'll wash them by hand. And maybe his pajama bottoms, too. They might have stains. You never know. What did you do with that bag of dirty clothes?"

Finally, we use the word we've been avoiding.

"He has leukemia, Mother. We don't know how long he has to live."

In the hospital corridor our four-foot-ten mother looks even smaller. She glances at us, her three scared daughters, and shrugs as if we have mentioned that a thunderstorm is brewing or there's just been a tax increase.

"So what are you going to do?" she says.

This is not a question about our plan of action, as in *what are you planning to do*? She is surrendering—at least outwardly—to a cruel reality of life in a *que sera, sera* kind of way. This is a woman who fusses over the high price of lettuce or cookie crumbs that might attract ants. Perhaps she has come to terms with that over which she has control—the spiciness of the tomato sauce, the cleanliness of our clothes—and that over which she has none. In the process, her unexpressed feelings get stored on a shelf, only to tumble out later, a trait I detect in myself and pray for God to change.

Her complete story has never been revealed to us, except that when she was very young—the youngest of eight—she was sent to live with an older married sister until that sister gave birth to her second daughter and had no extra room. She remembers that sister, the wife of a streetcar driver, buying her black-and-white shoes—high-top patent leathers—a luxury she would have never been treated to by her parents, who could barely afford food. When she returned home, after finishing eighth grade she was forced to drop out of school, either because her parents needed her help on their farm or because they couldn't pay the bus fare; I've heard it told both ways. When asked for details, she swats the air as if I am the pesky fly.

One time I asked Dad why he had married Mother.

"She knew how to cook," he answered, not joking. "And she looked pretty good."

According to Dad, they met at a party. "And a party in those days," said Dad, "meant a bunch of people getting together at somebody's relative's house." When they were both eighteen years old, my father took my mother over the Pennsylvania border into West Virginia, and he married her.

Now nearly seven decades later, she stands outside her husband's hospital room, presented with the prospect of life without him. Her white vinyl purse dangles from her hand, as if she has no use for what's inside it.

Something is going on here, a nudging, a gentle pushing. Thoughts are entering my mind, as if the Holy Spirit is turning the knobs. Thoughts that are urging me to pray with Dad. I can't do *that!* The only praying I've experienced with Dad is our blessing before dinner or the recitations in unison in church. I'm just *learning* to pray aloud with others. Clumsily, in fact. In the safety of Father Bill's office, with the cushion of other Alpha team leaders, I've merely tiptoed into this endeavor. Or with Alpha participants who *requested* me to pray with them, certainly I've obliged. Could Alpha have been God's way of preparing me for this very moment? Never before had I known the peace and strength that comes from a personal relationship with Jesus. Never had it occurred to me that you have to *do* something to enter into that relationship and that that something is so simple: Just ask. And Jesus will never say no. Does Dad know this? If he knew, certainly he would have told the rest of us, wouldn't he have?

Now here with Dad, it doesn't feel so simple. How would I start? What would I say? And if I offered to pray with him, would Dad perceive that I'm surrendering to his death, the same heartbreak I felt when he wrote those checks from his hospital bed? Surrender is not a bad thing, especially not to the God who loves us completely. The act itself of asking Dad to pray requires surrender. How will I find the courage unless I surrender my fears to God?

"Dad, would you like to pray together?" His hand is warm inside mine, and I squeeze it. He is groggy, weak, propped slightly in the hospital bed. Outside it is dismal, the sky a flat gray. "A prayer to affirm your love for Jesus?"

He nods.

Please God, please give me the words.

"Holy, heavenly Father," I begin, then pause to take a breath.

"Holy … heavenly … father." Dad's words are garbled, his voice barely audible.

I put my fingers to his lips. "It's okay, Dad, if you want to save your breath. You can just think the words as I pray them."

He nods, and I begin again. Syllables drift into the medicinal air, loose and sullen; my words fall askew like poorly strung beads. This is not easy. Never have I led my self-sufficient father in anything! *Turn it over to God*, I remind myself. *Turn all of it over to God.* And so the words of praise come for God, for his awesome power and love. The words to confess our sorrow for all the things we have ever done to offend him, the words to ask his forgiveness. The words of gratitude to God—and these pour out—for coming himself in the body of his son to bear the burden of our sins and give us an unencumbered relationship with him. Gratitude for the richness and fullness of Dad's life, for Dad's special qualities, his sense of humor, his immense love, his perseverance, his integrity, his faith. Gratitude for bringing us together this summer, for putting us here at each other's side. And then the invitation, the "please," to ask Jesus to come into our hearts, to stay with us and be our source of strength, to help us glorify God for the rest of our journey on earth and to bring us together again for the hugest family reunion of them all, the one he has planned for us in everlasting life.

At the end of our prayer, Dad opens his eyes and smiles. "Thank you," he whispers. He closes his eyes again. How sad to have waited so long to pray together. How glorious to still have the opportunity.

"What are you talking about?" Dad asserts. "Of course you should go!" Surely he is making Herculean efforts to sit up in bed and eat token servings of hospital Jell-O, trying to convince us not to change our vacation plans. It is hard to say how long this hospital will serve as Dad's home. The doctors continue their batteries of tests, none of which reveal reasons for his abdominal and back pain. Months ago Randy and I reserved the cottage we have come to love on the Chatham, Cape Cod, beach for our two-week summer vacation. On Friday we were to stop along the way to catch a baseball game in New Jersey. Then, on Saturday, we had tickets for *The Lion King* on Broadway. Now we wonder what to do.

On one hand, it seems impossible to think of leaving Dad. On the other, I feel that God is telling us to go, to rest, to revitalize and store energy that will be needed later. I have a strong sense of this. Randy and I discuss our options. Finally, we decide to forego the Friday baseball game and leave early Saturday morning. Marge will stay in Lancaster a bit longer. Pat will be here. We can check in with Pat daily and return home quickly, if needed. It sounds like a good plan to everyone except Dad; he is immovable.

"Why are you changing your plans?"

"I'd feel more comfortable being here, Dad," I say. "Just until we hear the CAT scan results. It's just a day. Plus, Randy can use the extra time to finish a job he's working on."

Dad turns his head toward the window that overlooks the Lancaster skyline. It is gut wrenching to see him not get his way, yet gut wrenching to leave him.

On Friday, we learn that his CAT scan is clear. His temperature has returned to niney-six degrees. They're adjusting his medication to alleviate the nausea. Friday evening we return from the hospital cafeteria—Mother, Marge, Pat, and I—to Dad's room. His door is wide open. And there he is in the bed, sprawled on his back, sleeping. His mouth hangs open and he is snoring—a deep, rippled whirling as free as I've seen since he was admitted here five days ago. God's voice of affirmation is so soothing.

"Will you tell him I said goodbye?" I whisper to the nurse. "And that I love him."

Chatham

The sheets feel damp under my legs, crossed Indian-style on the bed. Rain pelts against the windows—three, 20-inch squares—on the beach side. The ocean roars, slapping waves against the sand, a reassuring reminder that it is still there. It is good to be back in this aqua-painted room with its creaky dresser and uneven floorboards. On the wall, as if rolling in sync with the storm, hangs a painting of *Avola*, the sea captain's ship after which this cottage was named.

There is no air conditioning to drink away the moisture, but inside this room is a stillness and, before me, a Bible whose pages are open in a serendipitous way. This ancient book is new to me, and I am just learning to hear God's voice in it.

> *By the seventh day God had finished the work he had been doing; so on the seventh day he rested from all his work. And God blessed the seventh day and made it holy, because on it he rested from all the work of creating that he had done.*
>
> (Genesis 2:2–3)

The footnote says, "God demonstrated that rest is appropriate and right.... Our times of rest refresh us for times of service."[3]

God's love amazes me. The ways he finds to speak to me, the tenderness in his voice. How reassuring to know he has brought me here, both to this place and to this point in my faith, newly awakened just in time for this summer when I would be destitute without it.

Downstairs. Dibs on the reading chair, the most coveted spot in the house, an old green rocker-recliner that feels like a hug: *Hello, welcome back, where have you been all year?* The chair is tucked in a pine-paneled nook lined on one side with shelves of books, videotapes, cassettes, and knickknacks: a variety of ships in bottles, a miniature replica of a lighthouse, an old seaman's lantern, a brass figurine of dolphins rising from the sea, a collection of mugs bearing seashore images, an old sailing chart drawn in the 1700s. And there, straight ahead through the triple-paned picture window, is a weathered fence undulating onto the sandy beach. And beyond it, the ocean. All the reasons we've come here surround me in this space.

How many books have been read in this very spot! This year, my first will be *Evening*, a novel by Susan Minot, which happened to land in my suitcase, grabbed from a growing pile of books to be read "someday." This one, it turns out, God has chosen for me; the timing is too significant for it to be otherwise.

The main character is an elderly woman with a terminal disease. On her deathbed, barely aware of family members weaving in and out of the room, she dreams of the pivotal events that have shaped her life. The woman recalls asking the doctor how long she has to live and, throughout the story, the doctor's answer echoes in her mind: "Let's just put it this way," he says, "you won't be around to see the leaves change." [4]

It is early August now. As I think of my father, there is a foreboding connection with those words. *You won't be around to see the leaves change.* The words follow me on strolls through downtown Chatham, on my walks along the beach, forcing themselves to fit like a new pair of shoes. Within a day after our arrival, the rain stops. The first time the sun has shone in weeks, say the locals. And, as if peeking from behind the clouds, my mind begins to clear, too. It is now free to acknowledge the questions of my heart. *What will leukemia do to Dad's body? What will he feel as he's dying? What will I say to him? How can I comfort him?*

I long to find answers to these questions, but my research is futile. The medical books at Chatham's public library sound clinical. I am sick of hearing about blasts, the abnormal cells that never mature enough to carry out their normal functions. The blasts increasing, the disease worsening. We drive to nearby Orleans where the library books affirm leukemia's symptoms: fever, chills, weakness, fatigue, frequent infections, loss of appetite and/or weight, swollen or tender lymph nodes or liver or spleen (could this be the cause of the abdominal pain?), tiny red spots (petechiae) under the skin, swollen or bleeding gums, sweating, bone or joint pain. Check, check, check, check. Already we have seen many of these.

Absorbed in my searching, praying, and wondering, every now and then something startles me, awakening me from my dream. A waiter's question. A strain of music. And suddenly there we are, Randy and Katherine and I, sitting in an Orleans restaurant, twinkle lights strung like clothesline beneath a striped awning. On the plate before me, there is Caesar salad, wilted, a token array of shrimp. My appetite, like my mind, has also wandered away. Katherine is dressed in cut-offs and a halter-top. Her cheeks and nose, I notice for the first time, are sunburned. She is sulking.

"What's wrong, Katherine?" I ask.

"There's nothing good to eat here," she says.

"Well, what about your salad?" Randy asks.

"I don't like it. It tastes yucky."

"Well then, next time we won't take you out to dinner with us," Randy grouses.

Suddenly it seems there is no place to hide, no escaping this fretful dreaming whose boundaries diffuse into loneliness. Sometimes I forget about God. Sometimes I do not feel his presence. Sometimes I don't even feel like trying.

The bed's brass headboard feels cold against my neck as I finish my conversation and hang up the telephone. Apparently Mother had an episode today. They were driving home from the hospital, Marge and Pat in the front seat, Mother in back, when suddenly the emotion bottled up inside her exploded. She was angry about a dispute with my father before they left Florida, the details of which were too convoluted to grasp. Did she think that by railing about their differences, she could cement the distance between them and minimize the pain of her loss? My sisters, both captive in the front seat, could hardly breathe.

My heart is racing. Selfishly, I am too consumed by my own grief to make allowances that are needed. Downstairs in the kitchen, a ship's lantern above the sink gives off a faint light, and outside the window the night is dark. This room that usually feels cozy—with its knotty pine cabinets, its brick patterned floor—is stifling now. The crunch of potato chips echoes around me and, when I look down, the bag is nearly empty. Inside the refrigerator, there's leftover taco salad, vanilla pudding, a few containers of kids' yogurt, a doggy bag from the Chatham Squire. I'm not even hungry. I think I will read.

And so, again, the Bible sits open before me. A prayer card—given to me by an Alpha guest—slips from the page, as if when I absent-mindedly stuck it there, God guided my hand in marking the page for tonight.

> For Moses said, "Honor your father and your mother," and "Anyone who curses his father or mother must be put to death."
>
> (Mark 7:10)

It is surprising that the notes at the bottom of the page do not have my name on them. This is what they say: "Look to Christ for guidance about your own behavior, and let him lead others in the details of their lives." And: "God's law specifically says to honor fathers and mothers and to care for those in need.... Helping those in need is one of the most important ways to honor God."[5]

Now isn't that something? No place in there does it say to *understand* our parents, but to *honor* them. Nowhere is the command to agree with them or to side with them or to act like them. Just honor them. Honor them? As in not retaliate. As in not get so choked by my own miniscule understanding of another person's pain that I play out the urge to scream my head off and stomp my feet and spit. And help those in need? Sometimes God sets the bar so high, it seems impossible to get near it. *I need to know how, God. I need to know how exactly you want me to help those in need.*

The smell of books makes me feel liberated, the way some people breathe in ocean air and feel alive. It is good to be back in this quaint Main Street bookshop roaming the narrow aisles, inhaling the familiar scent of the printed word. The classics, the contemporary work; all of it invigorates me. Draws me in. Tempts me to take it home.

The topic for which I am searching, it turns out, is in the Health section, tucked in the back, next to the bottom shelf. My search has been much like the process by which some people shop for furniture, unable to describe exactly what they want, but when they see it, they know. *Final Gifts* is written by two hospice nurses. The promise on the cover addresses my yearning: "Understanding the special awareness, needs, and communications of the dying."[6] The cover's graphic is a border of green leaves changing in color to leaves of autumn, and there it is again, that thought returning like a whisper: *You won't be around to see the leaves change.*

The book fits comfortably in my hands; I can almost feel the angels who put it there letting go. Tenderly. Lovingly. There. For you. And I am left at the bedside of a twenty-seven-year-old cancer victim who, just before he died, sat up, pointed, and called out the name of a boyhood friend, who had come to take him swimming. Shortly after the cancer victim's death, his family learned that his boyhood friend had also recently died. The story is one of many that reaffirm an eternal life where we are not alone, where our bodies become whole and perfect.

Some stories tell of hospice patients describing in detail a specific place that they are seeing for the first time, or simply a light that they cannot help but follow. Other stories illustrate the need for patients to clear up last-minute details before they can let go and move on. Or to exercise what appears to be their option to choose the precise moment to leave this earth—such as right after they've said goodbye to someone, or after a particular person, on whom they wouldn't want to impose the burden of witnessing their last breath, leaves the room.

My mind is spinning. This information that would have been of no personal use and only of passing interest to me just a few months ago is now paramount in value. Randy reads the book, too. He is fascinated by it. Where are we headed? Why are we being prepared this way? Our journey is cloaked in awesome wonder whenever we trust that God is doing the navigating.

"Are you kidding? How can he be home?"

"He insisted on it," Pat says.

Pat and I had agreed to telephone one another every two nights during my stay in Chatham; so far we've held marathon conversations three nights in a row.

"He said to the doctor, 'Nobody's really doing anything for me here, right?' and the doctor said, 'Well, that's right.' So Dad said, 'Then why am I still in the hospital?'"

"But how can he be at home?" My mind still sees the pallor of Dad's skin, the constant tilting of his hospital bed to ease the pain. "I can't even picture this."

Pat explains that she and her husband, Ward, set up a hospital bed and bedside commode—ordered by the doctor—in the spare Valleybrook bedroom. She filled Dad's prescriptions and checks on Mother and Dad frequently, picking up groceries as they need them. Dad is starting to eat a little soup, a taste of ice cream. Mother even made him a pepper-and-egg sandwich, Pat tells me.

It fills me with hope to hear that my father, gasping for breath just a week ago, is now sitting in the living room, watching CNN or skimming *The Wall Street Journal*. Much of this, of course, we ascribe to Dad's tenaciousness; clearly, he is bucking the system. In short stints, says Pat, he glances through mail at the dining room table where the pile is bulging with statements and confirmation slips for the twenty-some investment accounts he manages for relatives. Since his arrival in June, Dad has lined the dining room floor with corrugated boxes, where he keeps file folders labeled in his tidy script: *investments, statements, receipts, "unfinished business."* One box contains the legal brief for a case he is slated to arbitrate next month in Fort Lauderdale. For years since his retirement from the construction business, he has served as an arbitrator for the National Association of Securities Dealers. One case that he arbitrated last summer dragged on through four 10-hour days.

Now, sitting in the Chatham cottage, I yearn to see him. If only I could speak to him. But Mother cannot hear on the telephone and does not answer it. And the distance to the kitchen phone from Dad's favorite living room chair is too much for him to negotiate. Pat and I discuss the possibility of installing a cordless, but Dad's energy is waning and he doesn't want to be bothered by talking on the telephone. His friends from Florida call almost daily, and it takes everything in him to pick up the receiver. His golf buddies are flabbergasted to find their vibrant friend breathless, barely able to sustain a conversation.

So I send Dad my love through Pat, assuring him that we are enjoying our vacation, when what we are really doing is wondering how soon we should return home. My heart aches at the thought of being away from him for two whole weeks. Randy agrees. We decide we'll head home on Tuesday. Upon hearing our decision, Katherine also looks relieved.

These are not tiny ants on convention at a crumb of food. They are the large independent variety making their appearance according to their own schedules. One from the cabinet kickboard onto the kitchen floor. Another on the counter not far from the cook top. Another next to the sink. Another near the knotty pine stairway. Bug repellent has not fazed them. Squishing their fully developed bodies under our sneakers feels akin to murder. Reached by telephone, the rental agent relays an explanation from the exterminator: After weeks of rainfall, it's not uncommon for ants to appear in search of a dry place. She offers to put us on the exterminator's list. We arrange a day and time. They'll set off a killer bomb beneath the house, she tells me, and we'll have to stay out of the house for at least two hours.

"But don't expect them to disappear immediately," she warns. "In fact, at first, you'll probably see more of them."

One side of me wants to shake my fist at God. *Don't we have enough to deal with? Can't you send the ants to someone else's cottage, maybe to someone whose father isn't terminally ill?*

The other side of me labors at sharpening my perspective. *What are a few ants? So it's a couple hours of inconvenience. A hiccup in the larger scheme of things. Not worth the energy to fuss about.*

In any case, my Catholic upbringing—or is it my Italian heritage?—keeps me in check when it comes to chastising God. It subdues my urge to engage in a tirade over the ant problem as a matter of respect for my father—both my father in heaven and the one on his way there. I close the cottage door, leaving the ants behind for God and the exterminator to deal with. It will be okay. Everything's going to be okay.

An overcast day. The sky is colorless, the earth without a lid on it. Please don't anyone be cranky or moody. There is a certain fragility to the air around me, as if it might crack at the slightest disturbance. I need to be alone. Do something mindless. Drive into town, buy anything I want. Cheer myself up.

Main Street's sidewalks are crowded with disappointed beachgoers milling single file. A large picture window displays pointy-toed shoes with high heels, trendy clogs, and a sale sign in script lettering. Inside the tiny shop are leather-cushioned benches where women with dainty feet slip on patent leather pumps or lace-up ankle boots. Stacks of shoe-boxes clutter the floor. The sandals worn by the sales clerk look comfortable. An earthy shade of sage green, they are unlike my own shoe wardrobe of black, brown, and taupe. The idea of treating myself to something I've never had be-fore—sage green sandals—intrigues me.

"Sorry," the sales clerk says, "we don't have any left in the sage."

It's okay. They weren't necessary. Just something to buy. If I want necessary, I should buy a dress for the funeral. Get practical. Think ahead.

Across the street is the Trading Post, swanky, expen-sive. If there's an occasion that justifies splurging, surely it would be my father's funeral. The door opens to the rich aroma of leather Ghurka handbags hanging on a coat tree just inside. There is mahogany everywhere: the display coun-ters, the railings leading up to the raised platform of cloth-ing racks, the trim. Even the hangers are heavy, dark-stained wood. The price tags: I won't even look. Just shuffle through the racks. Armani. Biella Collezione. Clothing cut for tall, glamorous women. I am short and ethnic looking. Nothing fits. You would think Italian designers would have a heart for women of their own nationality. Sophia Loren is short. I wonder where she shops.

The dressing booth is compact, a small wooden box without a mirror. On the outside is a full-length mirror. *Ugh.* Sophia Loren I am not. Witness the chunky hips, the wiry hair, the less than angular nose. I'll try one more outfit, and that's it. If it doesn't fit, I'm out of here. It's a Max Mara suit, whoever Max Mara is. Well. It actually does fit. Nicely. At least I'm not drowning in it. Three-quarter length sleeves, very comfortable. Neutral-colored linen, nice, not showy.

Not exactly a shade that comes to mind for a funeral. Does that matter? It wouldn't matter to Dad.

At the end of the day, a new sterling silver bracelet dangles from my wrist, and the back seat of Randy's Discovery is covered with bags. The Max Mara suit. Tall blue silk flowers in a glass vase with acrylic water. Ceramic coasters for Pat and Marge. Blueberry jam for Mother. A brightly painted piggy bank to be used as a birthday gift; surely one of Katherine's friends will have a birthday party soon. White capri pants and a matching sleeveless top, both on sale at summer's end. An oversized Tencel shirt. Two sachet pillows to be tucked away for hostess gifts. An onyx pendant in a silver setting. Whatever else is back there. Stuff. It doesn't matter. None of it does any good. Like a little girl who's eaten too much candy, I lean on the steering wheel of my husband's car, and the ache deep inside gives way to tears that fall on the new silver bracelet dangling from my wrist.

The lawn at Chatham's Kate Gould Park is covered with blankets and beach chairs. Balloons of red, yellow, blue, green, and purple float high and proud. Musicians tune their instruments. One couple has brought a picnic of Brie and crackers, grapes and wine, blue-and-white checked napkins, and peanut butter sandwiches for their toddlers. Next to them, two small children make their parents laugh with a Laurel and Hardy style routine. A father tosses a baby in the air. There is no place like the Friday night concert on a summer evening in Chatham.

For the moment, the blanket we've brought is mine alone. Randy and Katherine have walked up the path to Main Street looking for a glow-in-the-dark twizzler stick for Katherine to wear around her neck as dusk settles in. It feels good to breathe in this Norman Rockwell scene. It reminds me of a piece of Katherine's second grade artwork, a white dove mounted to a glittery blue background, and captioned, "Peace is when my family is full of joy and laughter."

The Chatham Band's leader tells a joke, then dedicates their first song, "Moon River," to a boy and his father whom the bandleader met at the fishing pier earlier in the week. The band plays on. There is no sign of Randy and Katherine. She is missing the kids' songs, her favorite part of this concert, which has become a tradition on our annual visits here. Where are they? The bandleader beckons the kids and their parents to gather around the bandstand, a massive white gazebo. Katherine and Randy are nowhere in sight.

"Come on, squeeze in tighter," bellows the bandleader. "Everybody now!"

You put your right arm in; you put your right arm out ...

The hokey pokey gets everyone smiling. Now the bandleader instructs the parents and kids to get in a line encircling the bandstand, hands on the waist of the person in front of them. The music starts, the bunny hop begins. The line coils 'round and 'round the bandstand. *Hop, hop, hop.*

Back on their blankets, little ones lean into their parents' laps. Droopy eyelids strain to stay open, as the band plays "When I Wish Upon a Star" and lulls them off to dreamland. On this crystal clear night under the Chatham stars, the music reaches to the heavens: show tunes, "Stardust," the "Blue Danube Waltz." Couples of all ages glide around the bandstand; some even waltz throughout the crowd. I love this place.

Finally, Randy and Katherine return. It is dark now, most of the concert over. The aggravation on Randy's face says *Don't even ask.* The gentle, loving father who built sand sculptures with his little girl just this afternoon has clearly been abducted. My daughter holds up a glow-in-the-dark stick that is *not* glowing.

"It doesn't light up," she frowns.

"Oh, no," I say. She is empty-handed except for the defective stick. "Where's your purse?"

Her face goes blank, then screws up into a grimace.

"I think I left it in the bathroom."

Randy's lips tighten; he looks about to explode.

"Come on, I'll take you." My feet hit the ground. The park is aglow with pink and purple and green glow-in-the-dark sticks. "We'll look for your purse, then we'll exchange the stick for one that works."

Katherine's hand is warm inside mine, as we walk up the path toward town, leaving the balloons, the families, and "Seventy-Six Trombones" playing behind us. The public restroom is behind town hall, a couple of blocks up Main Street.

"I hid it in a special place in the bathroom where no one will see it," Katherine assures me. She leads me to the stall, points to her secret hiding place—the top of the toilet paper holder—then bites her lip. The purse, of course, is gone.

"Oh, Honey, I'm so sorry you lost your purse."

"I hate myself," she says.

"I can see you're upset. We all make mistakes," I offer.

Inside the purse is her "vacation money," twenty dollars she earned from cleaning shelves, watering flowers, weeding. The purse, a woven black shoulder bag with colorful beads matching her flip-flops, holds other treasures as well: her red Hello Kitty wallet that she's had forever, her Beanie Babies club card, a dance recital photo of her as the itsy bitsy spider at age four. The notion of loss looms heavy over all of us. Like the ants seeping from the woodwork, it infiltrates our lives, showing up without warning. Silently, I ask God for a favor, a small one. My heart leaps with the hope that he hears me.

At the variety store, the clerk takes the glow-in-the-dark stick and invites Katherine to choose another. Outside, we head back to the park along the crowded sidewalk.

"Maybe we'll see somebody carrying my purse," Katherine suggests.

"Is the card with your name and address still in your wallet?"

"I think so. Do you think someone will mail it back to me?"

"I don't know, Honey," I say. "Let's just pray that the person who found it is someone with a good heart."

Saturday morning no one answers the telephone at Town Hall. Monday, a woman with an empathetic voice answers. No one has turned in a child's purse, but she offers to connect me with the police station. And there it is, waiting to be fetched at the Chatham Police Station: the little black woven purse with the red Hello Kitty wallet inside. And every one of my daughter's hard-earned dollars.

Sometimes God reveals his presence in the subtlest ways: the goodness in the hearts of others, his loving kindness that shines through them. I hope my faith grows even—or especially—in times when his answer isn't the one I asked for. For in my heart I believe that God's will always exceeds our greatest hopes. I need to keep trusting in that.

"He did what?"

"We were all sitting around talking at Grandma and Grandpap's apartment, and it was getting close to lunch time," my niece explains. The telephone in *Avola's* master bedroom is starting to feel like an appendage of my ear. "Then Grandpap said 'How 'bout I take you all out to lunch?' Next thing we knew, we were all at the Old Country Buffet."

"But who drove?"

"We took two cars," she says. "One of the guys drove Grandpap's car."

Why should it surprise me that this man, who barely has the energy to breathe, pushed himself to treat his visiting grandchildren—some from Pittsburgh, some from New Jersey—to lunch? Call it strong will; call it stubbornness. When my father is totally committed, as he is to his grandchildren, he simply brushes aside his own limitations. *Mind over matter, mind over matter.*

"He was leaning on the sign when you first walk in, the one that says 'Hostess Will Seat You.'" My niece sounds incredulous at the notion, though she herself witnessed it. "He could hardly stand up!"

From an outsider's perspective it must have looked like a man enjoying Saturday afternoon lunch with his adult-aged grandchildren. One grandson, solid as a fireplug, tells the story of how he once helped himself so often at a Chinese buffet that the waitress finally took his silverware away. "You go home," she told him. "No eat no more." Tears of laughter run down the cheeks of his audience—my father and his band of grandchildren. One grandchild concocts a sundae at the dessert bar for her grandpap who has always had a weakness for ice cream. Another returns to the buffet line again and again, piling his plate high, tickling the heart of his grandfather who delights in getting his money's worth. The laughter emanating from their table warms the room; the celebration of family is paramount.

God gives us beaches to walk upon, this much I know. Our sliver of beach at the end of Andrew Hardings Lane, in front of *Avola*, leads to Lighthouse Beach. The water is still now. To our right, atop the banks of rocks, sit gray-shingled cottages that inspire daydreams beginning with the words, "If I lived here …" It seems that Chatham Lighthouse, not far from where the water curves along the sand, will always stand tall.

Randy and Katherine skip seashells along the water's surface.

"Like this," Randy says. "Flick your wrist as you release it. That's it." Nothing matters to them right now other than whose seashell skitters farther, and that is a good thing. Not far away, a man throws a stick, and his golden retriever swims into the water to fetch it. It is a gift to be together here, yet at the same time walk alone. There is no extraneous clutter. Deep heavy breaths work their way through my chest; it is the most refreshed I have felt in weeks.

Where does strength come from? Like the rocks shoring up the land, strength is not the source of itself; it is certainly not its own creator. Why do we tout the trait of self-reliance when, in fact, it takes more courage to surrender to the one who gave us our self-reliance in the first place? Why do we tighten our grip in fear as if clenched fists are going to save us? The strength to be strong is ours for the asking—this, I believe—and it comes from a faith deep inside that gives us the grace to let go. With open hands, I tilt my face skyward and the warmth of sunshine washes freely over it.

At the tip of Lighthouse Beach, Katherine wades into the water. She looks back at Randy and me. We nod our approval, and she continues to a nearby sand dune, stepping onto it as though she has arrived at the height of Mount Everest. With both arms spread, she bows triumphantly, prompting our fervent applause.

A wind has whipped up, and the blinds are flapping against the bedroom windows. Waves smack against the shore. It is Monday night, and the news via telephone is not good.

Dad had an appointment with the hematologist this morning. Pat and Uncle Johnny, visiting again from Pittsburgh, took him there. At first, it seemed hopeful. Dr. Linley mentioned a new leukemia drug that's had some success in Europe. Then he left the room to view a slide of Dad's cell tissue under the microscope. When he returned, he was frowning.

"I'm afraid this is much further along than you or I would want it to be," he said. "I'm sorry. The drug is no longer an option."

Acute leukemia. The words we did not want to hear. *Hospice.*

"For you to qualify for hospice coverage," the doctor said, "I'm going to have to say we have no more than six months."

"Is that what you really believe?" Dad asked.

"Without a crystal ball, I just can't say."

"I would like to go back to Florida," Dad asserted. "Will that pose a problem?"

"Florida? Do you have family in Florida?"

"No, my family's here," Dad said. "But I don't want to be a burden to them."

The doctor glanced at my sister and uncle whose faces, I imagine, were wracked with sadness. Then he looked at my father and spoke kindly, gently.

"If you don't mind my saying so, you'll be more of a burden to them if you return to Florida," he said. "They'll be up here worried about you. To see you, they'll have to take off work and fly down there. And each time they have to leave, well, it will be hard on them."

"I never thought of it that way."

With five hundred miles between us, Pat and I discuss details, the only way we know to cope. Dad wants to have a family meeting, the five of us. He has formulated an agenda, many items of which he has already decided upon: to notify the holders of the investment accounts he manages that his services will no longer be available, to cancel his participation in next month's arbitration case. There are decisions to be made about Mother and Dad's condo in Florida, about their living arrangements in Lancaster. Their Valleybrook lease terminates at the end of the month—just a couple of weeks away—and the landlord is planning to reoccupy the apartment herself come September. We agree that Pat should call her to try to buy time. And as soon as I return home, I will start looking for another apartment into which Mother and Dad can move.

"He's not really taking to the idea of hospice," Pat says.

"Why not?"

"He thinks they're a warehouse for the dying."

"Did you explain to him that it's not a *place*? Their mission coincides precisely with what he wants: They help keep people comfortable in their *own* homes. You have to read the book I mentioned. *Final Gifts*. It's all in there."

"I know," she says. "I know that."

We agree to discuss hospice care at our meeting. In fact, for efficiency's sake—a notion that Dad embraces—we'll schedule an appointment with a hospice representative who can explain their services to us at the same time. We can convince him that we should at least listen before making a decision.

"Have a safe trip back tomorrow," Pat says.

"Our bags are already packed." Again, it is too neat and tidy that last week we chose Tuesday morning as our departure day. God's purpose for this trip has been fulfilled. I feel rested now and, though far from settled about what lies ahead, strong in the knowledge that God is with us.

Early Tuesday morning, we stop on our way out of town at Pine Acres Realty, the vacation rental office. I go in alone to return the keys.

"We're checking out of the Ganaway house," I say.

The agent looks puzzled.

"I'm sorry we have to go." Tears burn my eyes. "My father is very sick."

From the softness in her eyes, it appears that she herself has stood in my shoes. She reaches out and touches my hand. Her words are too soft to hear, but they are spoken kindly, and I thank her.

Six

Chairs

In a state of impending loss, I am starting to notice things
that never before piqued my interest. Like the chairs in
which Dad sits. Markers of his illness. The places he chooses,
or that are imposed upon him, to stop and rest along the way.
This morning, a Friday, it is a white plastic chair pulled in
from the Valleybrook balcony. Functional enough for a temporary respite, it is the kind of furniture that might be found
at a sidewalk sale in front of a drugstore. Not altogether flim-
sy, but certainly not a chair one would choose from which to
coordinate the final details of his life. Then again, Dad never
was a man of pretense.

With his cheek propped against his forefinger, his thumb
under his chin, and his elbow resting on the chair's arm, Dad
looks pensive as he listens to the hospice representative. She
is sharing the organization's philosophy on palliative care,
their goal being to make the patient comfortable, to provide the resources and sensitivities of a team well equipped
to navigate this path upon which we are embarking. The
woman speaks candidly, but kindly. She sits in Dad's usual

armchair, one with a sturdy caned back and blue cushioned seat, which he has turned around for her, positioned in the middle of the living room floor like a throne.

"I'm planning a trip to Florida," Dad tells her. This bit of information is offered most likely to test her reaction. "I need to get some papers, and I'll be hosting a dinner for my friends. Pat and Jan are coming with me."

"Well, we can provide a collapsible wheelchair that might make the traveling easier," she offers, magnificently passing Dad's test. "And I'll get you the name of a contact at the Deerfield Beach Hospice in case you need any help while you're there."

Another chair moved from its usual position, dark-stained bamboo with a thick floral cushion, has been turned from the dining area to face the living room. This is where my sister Marge sits, and after the hospice representative leaves, she is the first to speak.

"I don't see why we *wouldn't* go with hospice," Marge says.

The hospice agency would provide the staff—a visiting nurse, social worker, health aides—and the necessary equipment—walker, wheelchair, and bed. They would help locate suitable living arrangements for Mother and Dad and even offer a 24-hour helpline with the encouragement to call with any question rather than to wonder or worry. All covered by Medicare. It is an argument so tight that even Dad can't find holes in it. Just one important detail stands in the way: Dad's Procrit shots, a curative approach, is at odds with the palliative care provided by hospice, a fact that would disallow Medicare coverage. When Dr. Linley recommended hospice care, he never mentioned stopping the Procrit injections. Before leaving, the hospice representative offered to contact Dad's doctor for an opinion to help us make an informed decision. That handled, Dad is eager to proceed to the rest of his agenda. From the white plastic chair, he is straightforward and businesslike, albeit low on energy, chairing a meeting that none of us wants to attend.

First on his list: the investment accounts he manages. The account holders are all family members who have relied on Dad's keen judgment and generous assistance for decades.

"They are on their own now," he frowns. "You'll need to call and let them know." He recites their names, shaking his head as my sisters and I write them on our tablets. One does not know the stock market, he mourns. Another might have difficulty deciphering the monthly statements.

The case he's scheduled to arbitrate in Fort Lauderdale next month: Cancel. NASDAQ's phone number is in his black book. The Deerfield Beach post office: Call and have them continue forwarding mail to Lancaster until further notice.

In less than two weeks, Valleybrook's summer lease will expire. The landlord, according to Pat, has agreed to extend the lease through September. That gives us a cushion, but why delay the inevitable? We decide to start looking for another apartment right away. Two bedrooms, two baths, washer and dryer, a patio or porch.

"And the trip to Florida," Dad says. This is an item he has brought up repeatedly. He looks from Pat to me. "How soon can you go?"

Tomorrow! I want to offer, but Pat turns the pages of the day planner on her lap, rattling off a list of upcoming meetings and commitments.

"August 30th is the earliest I can go," she says. Today is the 18th. Twelve days seem a lifetime away, but Dad nods okay.

"I'll call my travel agent and have her book our flights," Pat offers.

"Call Esther Goodman, too," Dad says. "Claude's wife. She can set up the dinner at Crystal Lakes Country Club. She'll be willing to take care of everything, real nice lady. Just give her my credit card number if Crystal Lakes needs a deposit, but she knows the manager there, so he'll probably waive it. Ask her to also make the calls to extend invitations. Take down the names of the guests to be invited, will you?"

"Who's going to Florida?" This, at last, appears to be a subject pertinent to Mother. She has been sitting in silence on the loveseat next to Pat.

Dad starts dictating his guest list. "Of course, there's Claude and Esther …"

"Jan and I are going to fly down with Dad," Pat tells her.

"Who?"

"Dad, Jan, and I," Pat repeats louder. "He wants to get some papers and take his friends out to dinner."

Mother looks at Pat with the expression of an abandoned child.

"Lou Cordelli and his wife, Adele …"

"We'll take you down later," Pat assures her.

"But I have to get things," Mother presses.

Earlier Pat and I made the unilateral decision—perhaps selfishly—to alleviate the burden and risks by taking Dad on this trip, Mother on another.

"Just give us a list," I offer. "We'll get whatever you want for now, then we'll take you down later to get the rest."

"Reggie Wagaman, Milt Gordon …"

"Daddy has a windbreaker, a white one …"

Pat heads to the kitchen telephone to call her travel agent. Dad continues to rattle off names, which I scribble on my tablet while making a list of Mother's needs on another page.

"Chester Boyd, if he is back from Boston and feeling up to it …"

"And get my raincoat, the one with the lining, the good one I bought at Max Azen's …"

Today it's a wheelchair. The doctor's waiting room. Dad has just had his blood count checked, then his Procrit shot. In my hand is the computerized card with his blood counts. The hemoglobin has dropped again. Seeing my father in a wheelchair is no less frightening than what it would feel like to see him dressed in drag, impossible, embarrassing. There is not one thing about a wheelchair that matches his personality, not the handles for someone else to push, not the lock on the wheels, not the foot support, nothing. But there he is, confined, while the three of us—Dad, Randy, and I—await an answer that no one is willing to give.

The question is this: Should Dad abandon the Procrit injections, the only shred of hope he's been offered for raising his blood count, in favor of enlisting the services of hospice? By the very nature of its services—palliative, not curative, care—choosing hospice means giving up the fight, a decision utterly at odds with my father's tenacity.

Dad is adamant that the doctor, whom he deems the expert, render an opinion.

"It's just not part of their nature," a hospice nurse told me gently over the telephone. She has tried, to no avail, to get a direct answer from the doctor regarding the discontinuance of Procrit. "Doctors are about remedy, about treatment and cure."

"But what would he suggest if it were *his* father?" I want to know.

For a moment the nurse is silent. Then she says, "If I were you, I think I'd be as persistent with the doctor as you've been with us."

So on Friday afternoon, I called the doctor's office. Dad will be in on Monday for his Procrit shot, I told the nurse.

Could the doctor think about this over the weekend? When we are there on Monday, we'd like to have an answer: If it were *his* father in Dad's situation, would he have him continue the Procrit or choose the palliative care offered by hospice?

Now in the waiting room, ten minutes go by, fifteen, half an hour. Randy and I are making small talk. Dad sits in the wheelchair fighting the urge to doze. Finally, an hour goes by; apparently our question is the hot potato nobody wants to handle.

My incompetence at navigating the medical system haunts me. Every situation that requires assertiveness reminds me that we would be better off with Dad sitting in my chair and I in his. Something must be done. At the front desk, I talk to the receptionist.

"Excuse me, but my father is very tired. The nurse who you said would talk to us—could you check with her again, please?"

"I'll call someone," she offers.

In my heart, and in the hearts of my sisters, we yearn for the comfort that hospice promises, but how can we advise our father to fling open the door to his own death? We are cowards gone overboard with our sense of loyalty.

Finally, a nurse appears. She wheels Dad and motions for Randy and me to follow to a large open room where patients are stretched out on what look like dentistry chairs. Two patients are hooked up to IVs, one wearing headphones, the other staring straight ahead out the window. Another man, who is bald, sits sideways on one of the chairs, appearing to catch his breath before he rises. So this must be chemotherapy.

At the side of the room, the nurse locks Dad's wheelchair, offers Randy and me each a seat, then excuses herself to go get Dad's chart.

"Hello, Jan!" It is a cheerful voice. The bald patient. "Don't worry, we'll take good care of him!"

My face feels flushed with confusion.

"You are Jan, aren't you?" the man asks. "Jan Agnew, right?"

Nothing about this man looks familiar. But he used my former married name. He must be from the advertising business, a former colleague still referring to me by my previous name.

"Al Bustaque!" he offers.

A lump forms in my throat.

"Oh, Al!" I say. "Hello! It's good to see you." Immediately, my choice of words embarrasses me, but it's too late; they have already slipped from my mouth. In the early years of my advertising agency business, Al Bustaque was our sales representative from WLAN-FM radio. An extroverted Latino with a square face, a party guy. But now every blade of his smooth black hair is gone; he is astonishingly thin. Somehow Al still radiates cheerfulness, the way he always did, which makes me ache deeply for him. Before I can think of a more sensitive greeting, the nurse returns with Dad's chart. She pulls up a chair.

"How can I help you?" she asks.

No one, it seems, has considered our dilemma. No one has even given a thought to it. Slowly and careful not to reveal my frustration, I explain it to her. She is slim and pretty with soft brown hair. She asks questions, reviews the numbers on Dad's chart, then looks at him the way I must have looked at Al Bustaque.

"Hospice would take very good care of you," she says. "The Lancaster Hospice is one of the best."

The three of us sit in silence. Then Dad clears his throat.

"So you would suggest going with hospice instead of continuing the Procrit?"

"Yes, I would," says the nurse.

On the way out of the doctor's office, Randy pushes the wheelchair. Dad looks at the floor, his expression somber.

"Well, I guess that's the end of that," he says. If he is trying to sound matter-of-fact, his efforts are in vain. I remember what I asked him the first time we left this office—an office to which we now have no reason to return—less than three months ago. "When we pray for you, what do you want us to pray for?"

"No suffering," he said.

Please, God. Please.

Another chair. This one looks like a recliner, a bluish-gray velour piece provided by hospice, replacing Dad's caned-back chair next to the small glass lamp table. Its hidden feature is a hydraulic lift that raises Dad to a standing position without putting pressure on his aching limbs or back.

With the chair comes an array of other furniture and equipment, also at the order of hospice. The oxygen concentrator may as well be an alien spaceship with its buttons, knobs and tubes. How can I learn to operate such a thing when I have never even attempted to program our VCR? Without my patient husband, I would still be searching for the power button on my computer! Nevertheless, I am suddenly the designated head of the technical team. My appointment is purely by default, because Pat, an elementary school principal, works full time, Marge lives in New Jersey, and Mother has limited capacity for processing new information. Also delivered is a backup tank for the concentrator, suggesting the even more dire possibility of our losing electricity.

The equipment keeps coming, hauled in by two delivery-men traipsing up and down the Valleybrook stairs. As they do, Dad sits in the living room shaking his head as if no human being—terminally ill or not—has the right to cause such commotion. There is a standard-issue wheelchair, as well as the collapsible travel contraption promised for our Florida trip, a bath stool, bedside commode, bed table on wheels, and hospital bed provided to replace the current rental bed.

After they set up the equipment, the deliverymen explain how to use it. The pages of my spiral-bound tablet resemble a lab book with notes and diagrams. My head is spinning. In the spare bedroom, they tear down the original hospital bed, set up the new one. Mother stands in the hall at the doorway watching.

"How do you want the bed positioned, Ma'am?" The deliveryman—a husky, black man who emanates cheerfulness—smiles at my mother.

"She can't hear," I say. Then to Mother, slowly, loudly, "Mother, he wants to know where you want the bed to go."

"What?"

"The bed! Is that okay where he has the bed?"

"Oh. Push it that way a little." She motions toward the window. "See, I stand here and I peep in like this, so I can see his face without opening the door all the way."

The deliveryman moves the bed closer to the window.

"Like this?" he asks and then, in a louder voice, "Like this?"

"Here, let me see," Mother says. "If I just peep in from this angle. Sometimes the door's half closed, but I can peep through this way. That way, I can see if he's all right and I don't have to wake him up."

The deliveryman smiles a huge, broad grin. "Oh, this is just too cute," he says.

It takes a while before Mother provides a direct answer regarding her preferred positioning of the bed. She tells him how she changes the sheets and how, some nights, she sleeps on the nearby sofa wrapped in a comforter, no sheets necessary for her. She lets him know how she times it so that when her husband's in the shower, she pulls off the sheets and throws them in the washer, then puts on fresh sheets, you never know when he might dirty them. She mentions that one of her daughters bought soup in a can and that her husband likes that soup, she doesn't know why, it's probably just because Patty bought it, even though it cost so much more than her own homemade soup which her daughters told her not to put salt in anymore, no wonder he doesn't like it.

Suddenly I find myself missing my nephews, my mother's big-hearted grandsons. Like the deliveryman, they are charmed by the very behavior that arouses impatience in my sisters and me. Clearly, Mother is in need of attention, but my brain is so bogged down with the details of my father's dying, that my evil twin wants nothing more than to delegate her care to others—my nephews, the deliveryman—who have the compassionate perspective I lack.

It is not for lack of trying that my sisters and I have not connected with our mother. She has tried in her way. We have tried in ours. The trying just never seems to dovetail. It's like a latch on a suitcase where the top and the bottom are askew from one another, preventing the whole piece of luggage from ever serving its purpose and going anywhere.

One of my sisters never remembers being held by her. Another recalls Mother's slaps across her face. I was the youngest of five, her baby, adrift in the silence between us. Certainly there were tender moments. I remember, for example, sitting on the ottoman next to her living room chair watching "Lassie" or "The Ed Sullivan Show." She would rake her fingers through my wavy black hair, her fingernails perfectly manicured, painted a deep crimson red. Or riding the bus with her into downtown Pittsburgh to buy school clothes at Lerner's and afterwards, since I was good, M&Ms

at Kresge's, a pound of them measured into a white paper bag.

As I grew older, we simply never found a common ground. I didn't care about cooking, her favorite pastime. I still use spaghetti sauce out of a jar. She didn't acknowledge my interest in boys for fear that she might encourage me. She excused me from household chores to tend to my schoolwork—her way of wishing me well—and that was the extent of her involvement. Even now, I show her an essay I wrote, one I hope she'll enjoy about my late best friend whom she knew, too. She stands at my kitchen island, skimming the glossy magazine page, then shrugs her shoulders and walks away.

When Mother and I are apart, I dream up ways of bringing joy into her life. Like taking her to lunch, just the two of us, but the chatter in restaurants sounds like a herd of elephants stampeding through her hearing aid, and anyway the food's no good, she can imagine who's back in that kitchen cooking it, and at home you can make a whole pot of coffee for the price they charge for a cup. I think of sending her photos of my family, but what is she supposed to do with all this junk, she just got rid of old photos, now I'm going to clutter her drawers all over again. I consider buying her a gift, more junk, don't I understand it's not worth the money, all that Styrofoam in the box, that's what you're paying for, and the mailman leaves it outside the door for somebody to steal, you never know with all the workers, not to mention the neighbors nosing into everybody else's business. I think maybe, somehow, I can muster up the patience to sit across the table over a cup of tea and try to have a conversation with her no matter how much she diminishes me or the people I love or entire races and ethnic groups. But the minute we are in a room together, I am not feeling so charitable.

"What?" she snaps, as if I'm *trying* to not have her hear me.

I repeat my comment, no matter how trivial. The weather, her dress.

"What?" she says louder.

"Never mind," I say. It is almost too much to bear, this lifelong failure to communicate.

"You're just like him." She swats the air. "All of you! What do I care?"

One of my sisters, an educator herself, cannot earn enough degrees to make up for our mother's lack of schooling. And I, obsessed with language, struggling to be heard! But now she is about to lose her husband of almost seven decades, a relationship no one may ever understand. As she stands in the Valleybrook hallway, determining where Dad's bed should be placed, it takes her a while to communicate the desired location, but only she knows the angle at which she can see him.

We welcomed their idea when hospice first recommended the hydraulic lift chair. That was before we knew Dad's days of sitting were few. You don't think ahead to envision your father in a state so weak as to be unable to get out of bed, let alone out of a chair. In the end, the hydraulic chair will sit on display in the Valleybrook living room like a museum piece, barely used—maybe twice, three times. It will have just been a matter of days since it was delivered along with the other equipment, but suddenly it will be as hard to imagine Dad sitting upright in that chair as it would be to imagine him riding the Jack Rabbit at Kennywood Park.

Never Live Next to an Elevator

The rental agent jams the key into the lock. It doesn't turn. She forces the key, jiggling it this way and that. Cars whiz past on Route 222. Dad leans against the apartment's sheltered entranceway, somber, out of breath. He is in no condition for apartment hunting. We brought him here because the units available for September occupancy are few, and a decision may be required on the spot. But now it occurs to me that, after a lifetime of exposure to his opinions about necessary living conditions, I can almost read his mind. He is thinking right now, for example, that you should never live close to a highway, a thought that would have gathered less momentum had we been granted entrance to the other side of this door.

Mother's lack of hearing keeps her from deciphering conversation, what little there is of it. The nearby drone of cars exacerbates the problem. And even though there is nothing to share, Mother is undoubtedly thinking that no one ever tells her anything, rendering her confused and irked. Katherine is fidgeting, her face awash with boredom.

My sister Marge is uncharacteristically quiet, not even making her usual attempt at a joke, but I can hear what she, too, is thinking: *I can't believe this.* A pathetic troop we are, three generations of gypsies.

Still, the key does not work. The agent begs our pardon, perhaps the current renter, who is out-of-town, changed the lock. If we don't mind waiting, she'll return to the rental office and make a call.

"Can you hold on for a little longer, Dad?" I ask.

He nods.

Finally, the rental agent returns, the maintenance man close behind. He inserts the master key, but it doesn't work either. There's an empty two-bedroom unit two doors up, the agent offers. Even though it's on the second floor, and we need a first floor apartment, at least we can get an idea of the place. Dad inches up the stairs, hanging onto the banister. Behind him, Marge presses her hand against his back in an effort to make the climb easier. The apartment is spacious and airy. The agent explains the differences between this apartment and the first-floor unit, soon to be available. Marge and I try to communicate these to Mother, but with the dual obstacles of a literal mind and impaired hearing, it is no use. Mother shrugs and swats the air.

Dad expresses no opinion, and from the sounds of his gasping, it does not seem like a good time to ask. The agent is polite, patient; I wonder if she is silently questioning whether my parents would be better off in a home for the aged. But I refuse to relinquish the image of my vital father who is, I am sure, somewhere inside that failing body. Certainly he will bounce back; he always does. The agent promises to contact me when she gets the key to the other unit so that I can come back if I'd like to see it.

My dozens of phone calls have located only one other complex with a suitable two-bedroom apartment, though it won't be available until November. They're doing extensive renovations and, technically, they can't even guarantee the November move-in date; they haven't gotten a commitment from the cabinet guy yet. Dad is drained, so he waits in the car while the rest of us follow the next rental agent into a four-story building.

The apartment is on the fourth floor across from the elevator. Charming. A fireplace and, like their condo in Florida, a screened porch with a golf course view. In light of the leukemia, however, it is hard to know how Dad would feel now about living on a golf course, constantly reminded of the passion he can no longer pursue. Would he enjoy—or dread—sitting on the porch watching a long drive off the fourteenth tee? I have no frame of reference for judging this. What if I were dying and could no longer write another word? Would I still want to read what others have written? And what if I could never read again and there were books—beyond my reach—piled on a table beside me? The very thought fills me with longing.

Mother is nodding as she walks through the apartment, nodding and smiling. She stands at the door of the second bedroom.

"People can stay here when they come to visit," she says.

We tell her that everything will be remodeled—a new stove, new cabinets in the kitchen, new carpet, new paint, new bathroom floors. She nods again and says it reminds her of their last apartment in Pittsburgh. The agent mentions that a bank, pharmacy, beauty salon, and grocerette are located in the village, all within walking distance. We relay this information to Mother. She is sold.

What should we do? The tentative move-in date, Dad's feelings about living on a golf course. How can *we* make this decision?

"We have to get Daddy," I say.

It is awkward getting him from the car to the elevator. Marge takes one arm; I take the other. Inside the apartment, he moves slowly. He glances at the golf course. He critiques the quality of the material used on the walls of the screened porch. In the bathroom, he shakes his head at the cramped space in the shower stall, then returns to the living room.

"You should never live next to an elevator," he says.

Our hope is deflated. We are not making one inch of progress. Where can Mother and Dad live? No matter which road we travel, it feels as if some barrier blocks the way. Later, on the telephone, Pat reiterates the notion of leaving everything up to God. I want to spit into the receiver, not just because she is right, but also because the part of my faith with which I struggle most is trying to decipher that fine line between what God wants me to handle on my own and what he will take charge of without my assistance.

But, of course, there is no fine line, no rationale for determining what falls on either side of it. No point at all in engaging in a tug-of-war. God has a marvelous plan, much better than anything I can concoct! My role is to discern where God is leading, and then to follow. Only prayer can help discern where God is leading us, I know that. And maybe I *will* pray. Yes, maybe later I will pray.

The marketing representative's name is Lydia. How she loves working here, she tells Pat and me, it's just like family. In fact, the owners know the residents on a first-name basis. She does not stop talking as she ushers us, a brisk step to her gait, through the floral-papered hallways, pointing out a small living room over here, a fireplace over there, explaining that these are gathering spots for family visits. Lydia's disposition is as bright as the sun streaming through the sunroom windows, which offer a view of the parking lot. It is as if it didn't

occur to the architect that residents of this assisted living facility might sit for lonely hours in this circular room's wicker
furniture, staring out the windows, only to view the home's
cream-colored van and rows of parked cars.

Just off the main dining room, Lydia unlocks the door of
a smaller dining room. It is furnished with a cherry dining
table, china closet, and buffet. This room, she tells us, is available for residents who want to invite family for dinner.

In the new wing, the rooms are handicapped accessible.
As Dad's leukemia progresses, the bars in the bathroom are
there to steady him. There is help dressing, if and when he
needs it. His laundry would be done, his meals cooked. Pat
looks at me, hopeful. She appears to be buying this idea of
assisted living, while I am struggling to picture Dad living
among the elderly who use walkers and canes, inching down
halls toward the dining room, an all-day affair. But like Pat,
I can think of no other solution. It was Gwen, our hospice
social worker, who forced us to deal with the question we
were avoiding: *If they move into an apartment, is your mother going to be able to care for him alone?*

One recent night after ten o'clock, our telephone rang.
When I picked up the receiver, Mother shouted, "Get Randy! Daddy fell! Tell Randy to come over!"

"Okay. We'll be right there. It's okay, Mother," I repeated.
Loudly. Slowly. "We're coming."

Click. Had she heard me? Did she know I'd answered?
The phone rang again.

"If you heard me, call back!" she yelled. "Call back so I
can hear it ring!"

Randy jumped into the car and headed to Valleybrook, a
10-minute drive. Katherine was asleep in bed, so I stayed at
home. When he arrived, Randy could not lift my limp father
who, en route to the bathroom, had fallen on the hallway

floor. So Randy called our dear friend Dave, and the two of them lifted Dad and returned him safely to bed.

Now the offer of emergency call bells and assistance when needed is being dangled before us. A week ago, the term "assisted living" was not even in my vocabulary; we are taking a crash course.

Dad's feelings about "institutions" are paramount in my mind. Just touring this place feels like a betrayal of him. Still, we gather brochures filled with pictures of the lobby with its circular fountain and crystal chandelier, the bright and airy dining room. Before long, we are formulating a case to convince Dad that this should be his next home. We will need to emphasize that it's not a nursing home. In fact, those who need skilled nursing care would not even qualify for residence here. Lydia offers that, if Dad enters now, as the disease progresses he could remain here with the help of hospice and, possibly, private nurses.

With Dad, our approach must be analytical, well thought out. Money will be important. He would never stand for a huge entrance fee, and he is too private to divulge personal financial information. This place requires neither. We think we can get him to agree that assistance of some type will be needed; Mother—or any of us, for that matter—cannot provide the level of care he requires. One option is an apartment—which we have yet to locate—with a full-time nurse. The other is an assisted living facility. I gather the numbers and chart a comparison. Because cost is uppermost in his mind, it is highly unlikely he will agree to hiring a full-time nurse.

At his bedside, I wish I felt convinced. This is not a choice he wants to hear, but it is all we have. Neither Pat nor I feel equipped to accommodate the vastly diverse and intense needs of both our mother and father in our own homes. Not that he would expect such an invitation, but I want him to know my feelings, so I start there.

"If it were just you, I would take you to my home in a heartbeat," I say. "But you and Mother have such different needs."

"No, no," he says. "I would never do that." I can hear him repeating his philosophy on parents and the families of their adult children living under one roof. *There are too many discrepancies in living habits between the generations. It creates problems; it's a bad idea.* He has often lamented his own live-in grandmother being *pushed from pillar to post. She wanted to help and my mother—with good intentions, of course—wouldn't hear of it. "Go sit down!" she'd say. "Put that broom down!" I'll never forget the sadness in my grandmother's eyes. From then on, I was determined to never live that way—dependent on somebody else.*

Now I tell him how clean the assisted living facility is, show him the pictures. He brushes them away.

"It's not a matter of cleanliness," he says. "Many of these places are clean. It's the people who live there. They look like goons."

My heart knots with pain, both for him and for those of whom he speaks, living inside failing bodies.

"It's not a nursing home." I am a reluctant saleswoman. "It's more a place for seniors who need assistance with some aspect of daily living. Like having their meals prepared or knowing there's help nearby."

With this he does not argue.

"Let me take you there, Dad, so you can see for yourself. They'll even let you stay for a few days and, if you don't like it, there's no obligation."

"Okay, Sweetheart," he says, nodding off to sleep. "Maybe tomorrow."

It is no small relief to have garnered a "maybe" from him. In the living room, our hospice social worker and nurse have arrived. But Gwen and Jody do not share my hard-won sense of accomplishment.

"I'm sorry, Jan," Gwen says. "He may be beyond assisted living." And then she suggests the unthinkable. "If I were you, I'd check out nursing homes, just to be safe."

Suddenly the room is spinning around me. The hydraulic lift chair. The walker. The wheel chair. They are closing in on me. It feels as though my neck is stuck in their wheels. My breath is being squeezed from me. And deep inside is the fear that if I fall, the floor won't be there to catch me.

The woman's desk is covered with papers, stacks of forms. It has been a long wait in the lobby, and now here I am, hot and drained, with an official-looking nameplate on the desk smack in front of me: Admissions Officer. The woman is huffing and sighing, leading me to believe that our appointment is an intrusion on her day. She spiels off a list of requirements for a patient to enter this nursing home. Most of them have to do with money. She hands me the forms, pages of questions requiring answers I do not have. The telephone rings. She answers it. She discusses the details of someone else's admission. My father is dying, and the nursing home admissions officer is not even looking at me. She is talking on the telephone, chalking up another admission.

The forms are overbearing. There is not one question that my father would be willing to answer, none that I could answer without his help. How would I know his net worth? How would I know his annual income, the earnings from his stocks and bonds, his savings account balance? Are they kidding? Do they honestly think I'm going to ask my father these questions so that he can be admitted into a place that he has made absolutely clear he does not want to go?

The admissions officer speaks to me in dribs and drabs. The phone rings again and again. She takes every call. She conducts business, hangs up.

"Now where were we?"

She tells me that Dad would go on a waiting list; there may be an opening in two to three weeks. Meantime we should fill out the paperwork, submit the deposit. She will fax the necessary forms to hospice. Do I have any questions?

The woman's face appears to be growing. It is getting bigger and fatter. One of her eyes looks larger than the other. I am starting to feel nauseated.

"Why don't I just look around for now? Can you just give me a tour, then I will think about all of this?"

The woman shoves her chair away from her desk and exits her office ahead of me. She points to the dining room, rattles off something about eating schedules. She lumbers down the hallway, then opens the door of a room where a man with thinning gray hair is sleeping. She motions for me to follow her inside.

"Patients are welcome to bring their own furniture if they like," she says in a loud voice, as if no one else is in the room. "A favorite chair, artwork. But the bed and dresser have to stay. We wouldn't have anyplace to store all these beds and dressers."

To the admissions officer, this is a job; it is a place she frequents to hand out papers, give tours, field telephone calls. To me, that is my father lying there, rudely intruded upon.

Not far from a nurse's station is a place where patients gather to socialize. One man sits in a wheelchair, his head leaning on his right shoulder. A woman with stringy white hair and a disheveled collar sits in a chair staring into space. Another man in a wheelchair, wiry and gray-faced, is pulled up to a table. His head is drooping over a partially completed jigsaw puzzle, and he is fast asleep. The sight of him touches a nerve deep inside me, a place that is raw and sensitive. Tears stream down my cheeks.

"I'm sorry," I say, suddenly unable to stop crying. The admissions officer quickly ushers me into an activities room, empty now with chairs encircling a vast open space. She tries to show empathy.

"It must be hard," she says.

"I'm sorry, I just can't see my father here." The tears won't stop, and the one tissue that was crumpled in my pocket is already drenched. "He played eighteen holes of golf last month! This just isn't him ... *at all.*" I apologize again, because I have nothing else to say, and because I know that in my present state, I must be a marketing person's worst nightmare.

Outside on my way to the parking lot, there is a bench where I stop and sit to hunt through my purse for sunglasses. I have no clue, not even an inkling of what we are going to do. Yet leaning back, my face basks in the warmth of the sunshine. It is such a relief to have escaped that place. There is another nursing home to visit; maybe it will be different.

On the way down Lititz Pike, the late morning sun beats through the windshield. It is broiling inside this car with its orange neon '98 plastered to the front window; the air conditioning has not yet kicked in. On the dashboard a cell phone, which I've borrowed from Randy, rings. It's Gwen.

"Jan, how are you doing?" she asks. The very question chokes me with tears.

"I can't do this," I say. "There's no way I can put him in a nursing home. I started crying right in the middle of the place. I'm sure the marketing lady thought, 'Oh, isn't this just wonderful.' Gwen, there are people in there with their heads drooping onto jigsaw puzzles, sound asleep. It's just not him. It's horrible!"

"Yes," she says gently. "You know, this is all happening so fast. He's deteriorated so rapidly that you're not getting a chance to adjust to one stage at a time." Then, "I'm afraid I don't have much of a good report either. Is there a place you can pull over to talk?"

So, in the Freeze'n Frizz parking lot, Gwen's tender voice comes through the cell phone describing how Jody, Dad's hospice nurse, arrived at Valleybrook that morning to find him splayed across the bed, half-dressed. Even when sick, Dad has never been one to stay in nightclothes during the day.

"Did you not finish dressing because you didn't want to or because you couldn't?" Jody asked him.

"I couldn't," Dad answered.

The cell phone feels stiff in my hand.

"I think someone's going to have to be with him at all times," Gwen tells me.

Pat is working. Randy's working. Ward is working. Marge has returned home to New Jersey. Mother is nearly deaf. And I'm out looking at nursing homes. Everything seems impossible.

"Look, why don't I just wait here, while you go to your other nursing home appointment?" Gwen offers.

It is a relief to have someone do my thinking for me.

The admissions director at the next nursing home is in her sixties, older than the one at the first. It is obvious—red, puffy eyes, shaking hands—that I am distraught. It is clear— "I don't even know why I came here," I tell her—that I have no intention of placing my father in a nursing home. But this woman makes the kindest gesture. She takes me into the back of the chapel, and we sit there side by side, and she listens. She listens to me talk about how vibrant Dad was as recently as a month ago. She hears me spout off about the insensitivity of her counterpart in the previous nursing home I visited. She listens to the story of how, for the first time, Dad and Mother came to Lancaster for an entire summer, how this has to be a God thing—it can't be a coincidence—how I wish I could just let go and rely on my faith.

The woman is holding my hand now. She tells me how hard it was when she lost her own parents, how even though it is the right sequence—parents going before their children—you're never quite ready to let go.

"You know," I say before leaving. "While I'm here, I might as well look around."

So we walk through the halls of this home inhabited primarily by elderly Mennonites. There are Amish quilts in bedrooms, women in the dining room wearing prayer caps, men with long white beards. If there were a nursing home for Dad, it would be one where all his golf buddies were gathered. Sick or not, he would see them not as their illnesses but for who they are, because friendship equips us to do so. Wouldn't that be the ideal way? Reggie Wagaman with a twinkle in his eye, telling my father a joke. An old foursome reminiscing about the birdie that outsmarted a dogleg or the shot from the sand trap that landed smack on the green. People not bound together by their illnesses, but by the relationships they established when they were loving life, when they were the way they will see themselves forever.

Gwen stands near the refrigerator, two feet from where I'm leaning against the doorjamb of the Valleybrook kitchen. Her dark gray hair is cut short around her earnest face. Her skirt and vest are of a quality that flows softly, yet still exudes professionalism. We're speaking in hushed tones, not that Dad can hear us from his room a few steps away; the oxygen concentrator rumbles and spits in the hallway outside his room. A long tube from this alien spaceship on wheels runs from the hallway into the doorway, swerves up the side of Dad's bed, and connects to his nosepiece. According to Gwen, Jody proposed to Dad the possibility of his moving to the local hospice facility, the Essa Flory Center. The center offers twelve intimate rooms, some with private walkout patios and garden views. Still, Dad's perception of any such institution as a "warehouse for the dying" remains staunch.

"I want to stay here," he told Jody.

So the plan at the moment on this Friday, August 25th, is to keep Dad at home and hire private duty nurses.

"But what is *home*?" I ask Gwen. "I don't even know what I'm looking for anymore. Am I back to hunting for a two-bedroom apartment?"

"How long do you have this place?" she asks.

"The landlord said we can keep it through September."

"By that time, in all honesty, I think you'll be looking for a one-bedroom place."

"You mean for just my mother?"

Gwen nods.

"*Really?*" Suddenly it seems we've been robbed of months. Just two weeks ago, the doctor's prognosis was six months!

"Let's ask Jody what she thinks," Gwen says.

When Jody enters the kitchen, Gwen relays our conversation, and Jody nods in agreement.

He won't be around to see the leaves change. Unlike hospice, I have no reference point for how close the end is, but those words won't be shaken from my mind.

Gwen dials the telephone in the Valleybrook kitchen. She asks about the availability of nurses. Leaves our phone number. She hangs up, dials again. There are no nurses available. Anywhere. We are left with the hope that one of the various agencies she's called will get back to us if one of their nurses has a cancellation. At my father's bedside, Gwen asks, "Do you think you will be all right overnight with just your wife here?"

And, of course, Dad says yes. There are countless times I've been tempted to take Jody or Gwen aside to qualify Dad's answers, to reiterate the fact that it's just not in him to think of imposing. They must hear this all the time, the well intentioned interpretations of family members grappling to keep some measure of control the only way they know how. *He says this, but he means that. She would never tell you this herself, but ...*

It has become noticeably easier—ever since the hospice staff has settled in—to sweep away the nonsense. Their kind-yet-candid approach makes me wonder how family life might have been had we had hospice personnel to usher us the whole way through. Certainly we'd have garnered better practice at expressing our feelings, not stymied with worry about hurting, offending, or annoying. Perhaps we'd have been more adept at delivering and handling bad news. Could we have avoided our tendencies toward avoidance? Or waylaid our dubious protection of one another, and built up a trust not merely out of kinship but also on truth? What a tragedy it seems that the services of hospice aren't available until the end, when the lessons they teach could enhance a lifetime.

With no nurses available, we split the weekend into shifts. Pat, Ward, Randy, and I slot times for helping Mother and tending to Dad's needs at Valleybrook. Yet much of the weekend there are two or three or all four of us there with Mother and Dad. Nothing else on our calendars seems to be as pressing. Now and then we take breaks to rejuvenate. Randy attends a healing conference at St. Thomas. A little while later, Pat leaves to join him there. Ward sits on the balcony reading. When Pat returns, she takes Mother to mass at St. John Neumann, the nearby Catholic church.

Dad barely leaves his bed now. The impossibility of his making the trip to Florida becomes painfully apparent. Just the other day, Gwen forced the issue.

"Have you thought about what you will do if you and your sister get down there with him and aren't able to get him back?" she asked.

"The thought crossed my mind," I said.

So Pat and I decided to go without him, to get the papers he wants from his safe deposit box and to host the dinner party planned for his friends. Though clearly disappointed, Dad nodded in agreement.

Now at his bedside, his arm is warm to my touch.

"I'm sorry you won't get to see your friends," I say. "It must be hard being up here away from them."

He shrugs, then nods.

"Is there anything you want me to tell them when we see them at the dinner?"

"Yes," he says. "Let me think about it for a minute." He closes his eyes. In my spiral-bound tablet, pages of notes are scribbled: how to set the oxygen concentrator, operation of the emergency back-up concentrator, the phone numbers for hospice, the names of rental agents, features of the apartment complexes, retirement communities and nursing homes I've visited. In less than two weeks, every last page of this tablet will be filled: directions to the Pittsburgh funeral home, names of the newspapers in which the obituary will appear, *in lieu of flowers the family requests donations to Hospice of Lancaster County*, the thoughts I will express at the funeral mass.

Dad opens his eyes and starts to dictate, slowly, thoughtfully. He stops after each phrase, catches his breath, then continues. His words find their way to a page in my tablet. "My wife and I enjoyed all the wonderful years we spent at Century Village and are appreciative of all the many good friends

we made while there. I want to wish them God's every blessing and many good years at Century Village."

It is hard not to love this man.

Saturday night. Huddled at the edge of our neighbors' kitch-
en, it feels good to be back in the company of friends. Tony
is sautéeing the ingredients for one of his sumptuous pasta
dishes: shrimp, asparagus, and bacon. The women are wearing silk or rayon or crisp cotton blouses, while my tee shirt
and shorts are wrinkled and tired looking. Even though we
live just two houses away on the cul-de-sac, the thought of
changing the clothes I've been wearing all day at Valleybrook
felt like too much of an effort; and to my friends, I knew, it
wouldn't matter.

Tonight is Patty and Tony's annual "Pasta Bowl" party.
Randy and I were drained, but decided to drop in anyway
just to get a taste of life as usual. Instead, I feel like a refugee
pulling my friends onto a foreign land, with nothing to offer
but a glimpse of the rocky landscape. I tell them about my
futile search: the apartments, the assisted living facility, the
nursing homes, the nonexistent nurses.

"They offered him the Essa Flory Center, but he won't
go," I say. "He has this picture in his mind of hospice as a
warehouse for the dying."

"Oh, you're kidding," MG says. A part-time hospice nurse
herself, my friend's voice is the audible equivalent of two
arms reaching out. "The Essa Flory Center is like living in
the lap of luxury! It's beautiful!"

"Really?"

"Yes! It's where I'd want *my* parents to be if they were dying. *I'd* want to go there if I were dying!"

Her brown eyes are steadfast, sincere. There is no way not
to trust her.

"Tell your Dad to go," she says. "He'll be so well taken care of there; there's so much attention and love. In fact, it was seeing the Essa Flory Center that convinced me to work for hospice in the first place."

At last, a possibility. A glimmer of hope. Dad knows MG; she has endeared herself to him. Perhaps I can convince him based on MG's endorsement.

My neighbors take in the details of Pat's and my upcoming trip to Florida. The papers Dad wants us to bring back, the dinner we'll be hosting for his friends. And for the first time, I hear myself expressing my deepest fear about the trip.

"I don't know what I'll do if he goes while I'm gone."

"He'll wait," MG says. She seems sure of it, and her assertion echoes the stories in *Final Gifts*, the book I read in Chatham. They were stories of patients who needed to know that certain tasks had come to completion before they could move on, situations that suggested that the dying, in some uncanny way, choose the actual time at which they will go. "I know he'll wait."

"Your father is such a dear," another neighbor offers. Jill met him for the first time earlier this summer. A group of women had gone to the hospital to visit and pray for a twelve-year-old girl, a daughter of one of Jill's friends, who was in a coma with brain damage from a freak accident on an amusement park ride. Dad accompanied me to the hospital.

"It was so sweet the way he took Annie's hand and told her to hang in there." The memory of Dad holding Annie's hand is vivid in my mind. *You're going to get better. I know you will*, he whispered to the little girl surrounded by stuffed animals and balloons and collage posters created by her friends.

"Oh, I love your dad!" MG concurs. "He is so cute!"

Patty announces that the pasta is ready—Tony's specialty in an array of varieties—and that there are places to sit on the porch or in the dining room. But Tony's appetizers on which I've been nibbling along with a glass of wine have been dinner enough for me. Randy, too, is tired, and the babysitter has seen more of Katherine than we have lately, so we excuse ourselves and walk home across the cul-de-sac.

Half an hour later, the doorbell rings. It is a neighbor, standing on our doorstep holding out two plates of Tony's pasta. He is someone to whom I've waved occasionally as we pass each other in our cars. I don't know him well enough to know if this gesture is typical of him, but the china plates feel warm to my touch, and the stars are shining in the night sky behind him.

"Dad, MG says that the Essa Flory Center is like living at the Hilton Hotel, the lap of luxury." The image gives me pause—who wants to spend their final days at the Hilton Hotel?—but MG's voice is in those words and perhaps Dad's fondness for her will elicit a positive response. "Look, this is what the rooms look like."

The picture in the brochure shows a room with a queen-size bed covered with a floral bedspread. There is a brown leather sofa with throw pillows, an area rug over the wall-to-wall carpet, and a windowseat with a table surrounded by cushioned chairs. Through the sliding doors a large basket of potted yellow flowers blooms on a patio. In no way does it resemble a warehouse, the image to which Dad has adamantly clung.

"Of all the places, this seems like the best choice, Dad," I say. "We can come and visit you at all hours, just like at home. There are doctors always available, and it's nearby for both Pat and me—about halfway between our houses."

It is manipulative, I know, to use Pat's and my convenience as a selling point to a man with a strong distaste for imposing on family. At the moment, I can think of no other way to get Dad the level of care he needs.

Finally, Dad looks at me, defeated.

"Okay," he says, then he closes his eyes.

And instead of relief, my heart starts to crumble. He has succumbed to an idea that he emphatically opposes. This is not my father. His essence is slipping away. There is no choice but to face the fact that soon we will be left with nothing more than his lifeless body.

Gwen is silent at the other end of the receiver. It is the pause with which I have become too familiar: her prelude to bad news.

"Well, there are a couple of problems," she starts. "First, there are no beds left at the Essa Flory Center. The last one was filled just yesterday. The other problem is—and Jody is new to hospice so she didn't realize this when she offered the center to your dad as an option—he would have to qualify to go there."

"Qualify? How?"

"Well, for one thing," she says, "death would have to be imminent."

What does this mean: *Death would have to be imminent*? Does it mean in the next couple of hours, the next minutes? And who would *know* this?

"They would examine him," she says, "to determine if death were imminent. Or there would have to be some indication that the palliative care wasn't working, an urgency to change approaches. Quite honestly, I don't think he would qualify."

My fingers turn numb against the telephone. Nothing seems fair. Who makes up these rules anyway? Are there actually people who sit around conference tables prioritizing the nuances of dying? My God, I've never thought of it like that, but of course there are!

"If there *were* beds available," Gwen adds, "he could be admitted on a respite basis, to give the family some rest, but there would have to be a clear plan of where he would be going upon discharge."

An intense feeling of betrayal overwhelms me.

"Where are you now?" Gwen asks.

"I'm at my house."

"And who's with your dad?"

"My nephew. Pat's son, Peter. He came in from Connecticut today. He's going to sleep on my parents' living room sofa overnight."

"Have you heard from any of the nursing agencies?"

"Just one. They said there are no nurses available, but they'll keep trying."

"Well, why don't you get a good night's sleep tonight, and I'll meet you over at Valleybrook tomorrow morning?" Gwen offers. "We can make some phone calls. We may be able to find a transitional place until a bed is ready for respite care at the Essa Flory Center."

The next morning, Peter opens the apartment door in his tee shirt and shorts. His dark hair is disheveled, his face peppered with a day's growth of beard.

"Did you get any sleep?" I ask.

"Not much. Gwen just got here," he says, leading the way up the stairs. "She's making telephone calls."

We sit on the sofa for the typical debriefing between shifts.

"In the middle of the night, Grandpap wanted the oxygen tube out. He said he didn't need it, so I told him I'd lay it on the pillow next to him and keep the oxygen concentrator turned on, so all he'd have to do is put it back in if he needed it. But then I couldn't go back to sleep wondering if it was okay to do that."

"It was fine to do that. How's he doing?"

"Okay, I guess. He still has a sense of humor. Grandma went in to his room this morning and said, 'Did you know Peter's here?' and Grandpap said, 'No kidding!'"

"Would you mind staying a couple more hours? There's a meeting at our church I'd like to attend—I don't have to, but if you can stay, I'd like to go."

Yesterday, a friend at church invited me to a grief group meeting, held every other Monday morning at ten o'clock. At the time, seeking support for myself seemed extravagant. But now, listening to Gwen's futile attempts on the telephone to find a bed anywhere for Dad, makes me wonder how much longer I can take this.

"That's fine," Peter says. "My dad's coming over anyway to relieve me. I'm going back to my parents' house to shower and clean up."

At the kitchen doorway, Gwen puts her hand over the telephone receiver.

"There's a bed available in Ephrata. It's in a nursing home," she says. "The only thing is that it's a semiprivate room."

A fury rages inside me, not at Gwen, but at my own helplessness. Why must every available option defy my father's wishes? I will not do this to him. Deep inside, I know that if it were Dad searching on *our* behalf, he would not settle for second best, not for any of us.

"No!" I tell Gwen. "He wouldn't even want a semiprivate room in a hospital, let alone in a nursing home!"

She gets back on the telephone and speaks in a straightforward voice. "That's not an option."

"I've got to get out of here," I say. The day after tomorrow, Wednesday afternoon, Pat and I will board a plane for Florida. We can't leave our parents at Valleybrook alone. What will we do? With my purse on my shoulder, I head for the door. "I'll be back in an hour or two."

At St. Thomas, our pastoral care minister is leading the grief group. In Mildred's office, there are faces I recognize and love. People who understand loss. Four women who have lost their husbands, two at relatively young ages. A priest who knows what it's like to lose a beloved father. Mildred herself, as a child, lost her mother. They have all gathered in this group before, I am not sure how often. It is not difficult to settle in here; the air is full of belonging. As soon as I open my mouth, I begin to cry. Sob. Uncontrollably. Somehow through the tears and frustration I am able to describe my futile search for a place for my father to live. Finding a place should be doable, yet I am failing, failing miserably. The truth is, it is so much more than a place for my parents to live for which I've been searching. It is a place for my father to die, and as I say this aloud, I realize I need to ask for God's help.

In a soft voice, the voice of an angel, someone asks this: "Can they move to your house?"

"I've thought about it," I say.

Here in the safety of Mildred's office, the face of Jesus is reflected in every one of these people who have been where I am now. I cannot escape the loveliness in that voice: *Can they move to your house?*

The conversation weaves in and out from anguish to heartbreak to hope. One woman shares that years ago her nephew hung himself in his college dorm room. She still thinks about him, she tells us, worries about his afterlife.

"I believe that Jesus more than anyone else knows the heartache he must have suffered," offers one. "He would have compassion."

Others nod in agreement.

Another woman recalls the long road her late husband traveled before accepting Jesus. She remembers sitting on the edge of his bed at the end, as he lay in a coma, having lost all bodily functions except his hearing. She tells us of his out-stretched hand, the reaching motion of his fingers.

"I asked him, 'Have you seen Jesus?' And he smiled. Then, because we liked to kid around, I asked, 'Are his eyes as blue as I envision them?' To that he didn't respond. I guess he didn't like my joke. So I asked, 'Is heaven as wonderful as I think it is?' He smiled and smiled and smiled. Then he opened his eyes, and I knew he was nine-tenths of the way there."

My mind begins to wander. I am picturing Daddy now, resting in my sunroom. Mother, sleeping across the hall in the guest room. It will be a temporary move for Mother; I can explain this to her. Afterwards, we will find her a place of her own.

But for now, Dad will have me nearby whenever he needs me. And Randy—with his studio in the carriage house directly behind our home—will be close enough to help with the more private aspects of Dad's personal care. Katherine can help cheer her grandfather whenever he's up to it. And other family members can flow in and out at their leisure, with plenty of room to accommodate them.

Today is Monday. Pat and I leave on Wednesday for Florida. We'll move them tomorrow. Marge, I am sure, will come from New Jersey to keep watch over Dad with Randy and Katherine and Mother while we are gone. In my mind, I am moving furniture, imagining a room that is fit for the love of my father. Yes, this feels right. It must be what God intended.

EIGHT

Asphalt Shingles

S tand up now, Sweetheart." Her muscular arms suggest that Dad isn't the first patient she has maneuvered from a gurney into a chairlift. The ambulance has been backed into our driveway, and its rear doors are open toward our front door. Dad is dressed in short-style pajamas, socks, slippers, and a windbreaker, an outfit about which he apparently had little input. His hairy, bird-like legs are losing their tan. When did they get so thin? On his neck is a medicated patch to alleviate the dizziness.

"Don't worry, I won't drop you. Both arms around my neck, that's it, just like we're dancing. Come on, now dance around to the right a little. No, no, this way, Honey. That's it."

"He doesn't trust us," chuckles the other ambulance worker, also a hefty woman. "The whole way down the stairs at Valleybrook, we couldn't get him to stop holding onto the banister. We told him, 'Just let go! Relax!'"

The flagstone step off our front porch feels cool to my bare feet. *I wouldn't trust you either,* I am thinking. It is painful to see my father stripped of his dignity.

Earlier today, after Randy and I had rearranged the sunroom in preparation for Dad's arrival, I sat on the hospice-provided bed, trying to get a sense of what Dad's view would be. The head of the bed leans against the solid wall— the only one in the room without windows—on which hangs a framed Bart Forbes poster of an Amish woman in a crisp white bonnet. To the left, built-in bookshelves with mullioned glass doors hold family photos, books of artwork, clocks, crystal decanters. Five arched windows offer a view of the tiny stitch of property to the side of our home. Armstrong pines, rhododendron bushes, a dogwood tree, and hollyhocks brush against the windows, providing a screen between our home and those of two neighbors on the cul-de-sac, though still visible are a slice of roof here, a window there.

A folding rattan screen brought up from the basement provides privacy for the bedside commode. On the adjacent left wall, French doors lead to the hallway, across which is the guest room where Mother will sleep. Behind Dad's bed, in the right corner, another glass-paned door leads to our dining room. It is in this corner that the oxygen concentrator and bedside commode have been tucked.

The sofa Dad faces sits catty-corner in front of two of the arched windows. Its cushions are a spray of rose, sage, and taupe flowers against a periwinkle background. In the other corner—on the left—is a cherry-framed club chair and ottoman with large, down-filled cushions. A matching chair for visitors sits next to Dad's bedside, on the right.

This is what I see when I sit in Dad's bed, but what will he see? How can I know? Never have I felt what he feels, never have I suffered what he suffers. But Jesus has. Now more than ever, it is Jesus whom we need. *Please, dear Jesus, let us feel your presence.*

"People say, 'He's eighty-six, he's had a good life,'" Randy says. "But what they don't understand is who your dad is to us. He could be a hundred and six, and we still wouldn't be ready to let him go."

It is one of the kindest things my husband has ever said to me.

Settled into his bed with the back slightly propped, Dad points to a window.

"I have a suggestion," he says. His tongue seems loose in his mouth, his speech garbled. He is saying something about the windows or the shades that curve down from the arch and release by a cord.

"What did you say, Dad?"

"When you redecorate this room … "

The rest of his words are indecipherable, but it tickles me to hear Dad offering an opinion on decorating, which has always been an interest of mine, not of his.

"It'll only cost three, four hundred dollars," he says.

"I want to know what you're saying, Dad; I can't understand."

With my arm resting on the bed, I lean closer to him. He repeats his words, but still they are garbled. Does he realize this?

Again and again he repeats his advice; again and again, I cannot understand. Not that Dad and I share the same decorating taste, but unlike the times when I've dug in my heels at his unsolicited advice, now every word he offers is precious. His generosity overwhelms me, and I want to honor it.

Later, he points toward the window again. It is twilight now. Dad is talking about a fellow who, he says, is standing there.

Thinking it might be a neighbor, I look through the window. No one is there.

"Who is the man, Dad?"

"I don't know, that's what I was wondering." His words are still slurred, but by leaning in closer, I can decipher some of them. "… a fellow wearing khaki clothes … standing over there looking out the window. For about forty-five minutes now."

My father's voice is matter-of-fact. This is a man whose credibility with me has been solid; it is hard not to believe him. The book I read in Chatham, *Final Gifts*, comes to mind, the stories of visions, hallucinations. Dad's vision is real to him, which makes it real to me, as well.

Dusk settles into the sunroom, and Dad is still chitchatting. Randy and I make every effort to understand the things that seem important to him.

"There's a large abundance of asphalt shingles on that roof over there," he says. He points at the house next door, or the one next to it, I'm not sure which. Is there an abundance of shingles? What does that mean? If I were a builder, as Dad once was, would this make sense to me? He has always had the critical eye of someone passionate about the quality of his work: *The risers on those steps are too steep*, he would say, *the mitering on that corner is off by a fraction.* Now on the threshold of eternal life, it is reassuring to see the essence of my father linger on. He points to the other corner of the room, to the windows behind the sofa.

"What is it, Dad?"

"Over there," he says. "Those three bunnies."

Is he in the woods now? Are there mountain ranges, glorious autumn leaves? He seems in awe of the bunnies, which makes me joyful, too. It is as if we are on a trip through Port Allegheny again, Dad pulling the car over to point out the wonders along the way.

Eight o'clock at night. Dad has been talking since he arrived here at two. Often when he begins to speak, Randy or I hop up from the chair or sofa and lean over his bed, trying to decipher his garbled words. He has not napped at all, unlike the past week, when he slept more hours than he was awake. Mother is puttering in the kitchen, occasionally stopping by to take a look or to sit for a moment. Randy and I take turns sitting with Dad, concerned about leaving him alone.

He starts to get out of bed, as if he forgets that he needs a walker and someone to accompany him. Randy lunges to guide him by his elbow; there was no place special he was headed. Something is different here. Something is wrong. Finally, we call hospice.

The on-call nurse arrives and sits at Dad's bedside.

"How are you doing, Mr. Coco?" she asks.

"Much better now that you're here."

She has an Italian last name. Dad notices this on her nametag and taps it with his finger. They bond immediately.

"Do you know what day it is?" Tanya asks.

"Why yes, it's Monday," he says.

"No," she says gently. "It is Wednesday."

"Actually," I say, "you're both wrong. Today is Tuesday."

The three of us laugh. Dad tells Tanya that on Wednesday—tomorrow—his two daughters are going to Florida. I explain to Tanya that Pat and I are going to get papers for Dad and to host a party on his behalf for his friends. She turns back to Dad.

"Do you know where you are?"

"Yes, of course. I'm at Valleybrook." He speaks with his usual air of confidence. Even when he is wrong, it is hard not to believe him.

"Actually, you're at your daughter's home," Tanya replies with kindness.

"No, I'm going to my daughter's house later today. My daughter Jan," he says. "She lives at Bent Creek. Right now I'm at Valleybrook."

Later, in the family room, Tanya tells Randy and me that Dad is probably disoriented from the move earlier in the day. Randy and I are famished—we have not had dinner—but talking to Tanya is comforting, and we chat with her for more than an hour, while Mother sits with Dad in the sunroom. Tanya assures us it is common for the dying to have hallucinations related to their life experiences: the rabbits, for example, bringing back his hunting days; the roof shingles reflecting his occupation. She tells us to call again if he becomes agitated or if there are any other changes. If he doesn't go to sleep in an hour, we are to give him sleeping pills. He definitely needs to sleep, she says.

At 10:30, Randy gives Dad the sleeping pills.

"Dad, I'm just going to rest a minute over here on the sofa," I say. Leaving his bedside, I collapse on the sofa.

"Okay," he says. But in less than a minute, he starts talking again, the mumbled words that can only be deciphered at his bedside. Does he need something? Is he just chatting? Leaning toward him once again, I make a futile effort to understand.

"Dad, I'm going to sit on the sofa now," I try again. "I'll be right here if you need something."

"Okay."

And suddenly he begins to wave.

"There's John!" he says, excited.

"John who?" Randy asks.

"John Ruggeri."

"Who's that?" my husband asks.

"Why, he used to belong to Churchill." Dad says this as if it must have slipped Randy's mind, as if Randy knew the members of the Pittsburgh country club where my father used to golf. "I haven't seen him in seventeen, eighteen years."

"What's he doing?"

"He's walking across the patio toward me. He's saying, 'Hi, Mike, how ya doing?'"

At 11:30 p.m. the hospice nurse calls to check on us. Dad has been throwing off the covers, trying to get out of bed by himself. The bed rails are up, but several times he has attempted to climb over them. Randy and I have been glued to Dad's bedside for fear he will hurt himself. Hospice calls the doctor, who phones in a prescription to the pharmacy, something to calm him down.

At two o'clock in the morning, twelve hours after his arrival here, Dad is still awake, still talking. He waves to his older brother and cherished friend, Carmel, who passed away eight years ago.

"See you next week!" he promises.

My eyes, which I have barely been able to keep open, now fill with tears. *Next week!* Never have I heard my father make a commitment he could not keep. The line between the believable and the incredible has diminished. Yet there is a feeling of elation in my sunroom, a sense of anticipation. Never would I have fathomed our farewell to arrive with such glorious fanfare.

Finally, Mother heads off to sleep in an extra bed upstairs. Randy offers to keep watch until the prescription delivery arrives, so I can relax on the guest room bed.

It is easy to drift off, drained, yet somehow reassured.

At 3:30 a.m., Randy wakes me up.

"Hon, he's asleep," he whispers. "Come upstairs to bed."

Wednesday morning my suitcase is packed and ready for a noon departure. The plan is for Pat to pick me up, then we'll drive together to the Baltimore airport.

Jody calls. Dad's hospice team has had a meeting and agreed we should take the patch off him. It is the medication, they think, that is causing the hallucinations.

"But this is the first time in days he's not dizzy," I object. "And you know what? He seems happy. It doesn't seem right to take the patch off just to quiet him down."

"His lack of sleep could lead to a whole new set of problems," she advises. "It can have a spiral effect leading to more complications."

"But without the patch, he's suffering. He gets that horrendous dizziness."

"Okay," she says, "we'll talk about it when I get over there."

My nephew Peter has come from Pat's house to say goodbye before returning to Connecticut. He, Randy, and Mother are standing around the kitchen island. Peter looks worried.

"Don't you think we should do what hospice says?" he asks.

Mother, anxious to abide by the rules, agrees. I am tired. I am cranky. It agitates me that no one shares my point of view. How can we in good conscience remove the patch and invite Dad's dizziness to return? Finally, I give in, but I refuse to do the dirty deed myself. Randy agrees to remove the patch from Dad's neck after Pat and I leave for the airport. Later on the telephone, he describes how it went.

"We're taking it off because you were hallucinating," Randy told him, "and hospice thinks the patch is what's causing the hallucinations."

"Yes, I was seeing a lot of things," Dad answered. His voice, I can hear it, was subdued, embarrassed.

If I could reach through the telephone, I would grab Randy by the shoulders, pound my fists on his chest. Why did he have to use the word "hallucinating?" Surely he must realize such a notion would humiliate my father! Why couldn't he have just said we needed to remove the patch to help Dad sleep better? Now I am sure that if Dad has another vision, he will not share it with us. Oh, how I want to know what he is seeing; how I long for each glimpse of the other side! And there on the other side, of course, is Jesus. Jesus with his forgiving heart. The Jesus whom, at the moment, I cannot fathom emulating, even for my dear husband's sake. The Jesus from whom I fall so short. The one who graces me anyway with love, a peacefulness that finally calms me down.

As Pat and I pull out of the driveway for the Baltimore airport, there is scant relief, knowing what we leave behind. Our dying father. Our sister just arrived from New Jersey, panic on her face as she scribbled copious notes, raised eyebrows when she saw the pillbox with twenty-eight compartments, the incomplete schedule of visiting hospice nurses.

"You've been here all this time; you know what to do," Marge said. "I don't."

There would be the added tension of a strained relationship with Mother. Mother has been busying herself washing bed sheets, preparing meals. Sometimes she just sits and stares. It is hard to know what she is thinking or feeling; the words she utters are primarily focused on bodily functions and soiled bed sheets. She reminds us often that she has never been at someone's side when they have died. It has always been a moment or two after she has left the room that they have gone. My sister Lena, my sister Dee, Lena's husband, Angelo.

"Angelo called me 'Mother' right before he died. It was the only time he ever called me 'Mother,'" she repeats. "And when I left the room, he died."

What does this mean to her? We cannot know. She merely shrugs and sighs, "Oh, well. What are you going to do?"

Now occasionally, Dad adjusts the oxygen tube in his nose. When he does, Mother thinks he wants to blow his nose, so she presses a handkerchief to his face.

"Here, Mike, go ahead, blow," she commands.

"Get out of here," he says. In her deafness, she cannot hear, and only after several attempts at helping him blow his nose does she recognize his pushing away. There is a sting to this interaction each time it occurs, a longing—at least on my part—for harmony. It is a sensitivity that invades my own marriage. The petty annoyances go away, but then there they are again. The same old thing. In his mercy, God offers encouragement.

> *They will rebuild the ancient ruins and restore the*
> *places long devastated; they will renew the ruined*
> *cities that have been devastated for generations."*
> (Isaiah 61:4)

Later, Mother touches Dad's hand.

"Do you know who this is?" she asks.

"You feel like an icicle," he says.

Dad doesn't know it, but these are the words—revised according to the way she heard them—that will stay with our mother.

"He called me 'ice-a-box'!" She repeats this over and over again with the kind of laughter that sounds like love.

The city streets of Baltimore are jammed with traffic. How have we landed in downtown Baltimore? Neither Pat nor I remember ever having traveled through the city to get to the airport, but this is where the Internet's directions have led us.

I typically fly out of Philadelphia, not Baltimore, so my dubious navigating skills are even less helpful here. Pat's sense of direction is similarly useless. At every block, there is a traffic light. At every turn, another line of cars. The clock is ticking toward our departure time. We stop twice for directions. We wend our way back to I-695, where traffic is at a standstill. There must have been an accident.

Pat zooms down her window and yells to the passenger in the car beside us.

"Excuse me! Is this the way to the Baltimore airport?"

"No!" the woman says. "You need to head in the opposite direction. Get off at the next exit and turn around, then go two exits the other way."

We whiz past signs that threaten to lead us into Washington D. C., as the enormity of our mission weighs on our hearts: We are on our way to fulfill our father's final requests. Like slapstick comedians, we are lost before we have even started. If both of us pray, surely God will hear us. There is no other way than with God's help that the two of us can pull this off.

Final Requests

The bank lobby smells new—modern pinkish-beige marble, neutral-hued furnishings—unlike when Dad brought me here to authorize my signature on his safe deposit box card five years ago. It was during one of my visits to Florida, around the time Dad's heart problems had resurfaced. The quadruple bypasses, the increasing need for nitroglycerin pills always raised to new heights Dad's astuteness over estate matters. The bank looks different now; they must have remodeled it since the last time I was here, perhaps upon one of its transformations from Barnett Bank to NationsBank to Bank of America. I hope this is the right place.

My sister and I are here to honor one of our father's last requests: to empty his safe deposit box and bring the contents back to him in Lancaster County, where he lies in my sunroom, frail; riddled with leukemia; watched over by our mother, our older sister, my husband, my seven-year-old, and the hospice nurse.

Images of authorities—IRS henchmen, bank officers—sealing the safe deposit box upon the death of its renter haunt me. How many times through the years has Dad impressed such stories upon me? He himself has helped to settle numerous estates—brothers, brothers-in-law, daughters, son-in-law—and has garnered some expertise at it. Even though my access to Dad's box is perfectly legal—Dad having wisely added my name to his box in anticipation of a need such as this one—rational thought is irrelevant to someone whose nerves are as frayed as mine. My deeper fear, of course, is one of failure: What if I let my father down? That is the notion clamoring in a back closet of my heart: the thought of disappointing him when his dying wishes are so few.

Pat hands me the satchel she's brought for carting the goods away, a canvas bag emblazoned with the Temple University logo, the school from which she earned her doctorate. She takes a seat in the waiting area inside the front door and opens her pocket-sized Bible, leaving me alone to face the authorities at the teller window.

"I'd like to get into my safe deposit box," I say, attempting to appear nonchalant.

A petite Asian woman, even smaller than I am, ushers me into the vault area.

"What is your box number?" she asks.

My fingers are tight around the tiny red envelope that houses the key. The box number is handwritten on the envelope, big enough to see at a glance.

"Four-forty seven," I say.

"Which side is the box on?"

"Umm." My eyes work quickly, skimming the box numbers immediately to my left "Right there," I say. "Lower right."

She opens a miniature file drawer that looks like an old library card catalogue. She pulls out the card numbered 447.

"Logan," she reads. "Frances Logan."

The signatures on the card are foreign looking. My God, we've come to the wrong bank! Will the woman press a hidden button? Will an alarm blast, identifying me as an intruder? My face, warm and flush, has surely given me away.

"Perhaps the box is on the other side," she suggests. She must be luring me into some kind of a trap, probably one set by the FBI. What kind of bank has *two* safe deposit boxes numbered 447? She motions toward a small room of boxes immediately to our right.

"Yes, maybe so. I haven't been here for awhile."

She pulls out another card marked 447, this one from a miniature file on the right side of the vault. There on several consecutive lines is my father's familiar signature, crisp and tidy, each letter of his name clearly formed: *Michael A. Coco*. Through remarriage, my name has changed, so I flip through the stapled cards, silently confirming that my signature is current. And there it is. I could kiss it. The pen feels cold as I pick it up to sign my name.

The woman inserts the bank's master key into the lock on the safe deposit box—the second Box #447—and turns it. Then she inserts the key I've handed her from the tiny red envelope. It doesn't turn. She tries again. Nothing. She pulls away and looks at the number on the door.

"Was it 447 or 1447?" she asks. What if she is preparing for the lunge?

"Four-forty seven," I say, barely able to breathe. "I'm sure that's the one."

She tries again. Click. *Thank you, God.*

Behind the closed door of the tiny room where I go to empty the box, my hands move swiftly through a pile of eight-by-ten-inch craft envelopes labeled neatly in my father's printing. All capital letters. LAST WILL & TESTA-MENT. DURABLE POWER OF ATTORNEY. REVO-

CABLE TRUST. CENTURY VILLAGE CONDO. There is also a thin, black ledger whose first page states: *What My Family Needs to Know*. It contains account names, numbers and locations, policy numbers, the names, addresses, telephone and facsimile numbers of various attorneys, CPAs, stockbrokers. Until this very moment, I never viewed my father's obsession with details as an intense form of love.

Finally, the weight of the envelopes inside the Temple University satchel is on my shoulder. The woman takes the empty box from my hands, far lighter than when she first gave it to me: the ultimate evidence.

When I return to the lobby, Pat is still reading her pocket-sized Bible.

"Let's go," I say, urgent to escape.

She looks up, clueless.

"But it's raining," she says. "What took you so long?"

"Now!" I grimace through my teeth.

We are two criminals escaping through raindrops to the getaway car, a silver Camry rental similar to the one Pat drives at home. My heart is beating out of control as I jump into the passenger seat. As Pat drives out of the parking lot, I recount in detail my near-foiled attempt. She laughs with the ease of a woman still basking in the words of a pocket-sized version of the Bible, a woman who never once had a doubt.

"There was *what* flying around in the dining room?"

"Bees," Randy repeats. The telephone receiver feels sticky to my sweating hand. "Sixty or seventy of them!"

"How did they get in there?"

The image is surreal: Dad hooked up to the oxygen concentrator in the sunroom adjacent to our dining room and Marge, who is allergic to bees, frantic in the knowledge that a bee sting might threaten her life.

"They built a nest in the drywall next to the window. The high window. Then they chewed a hole through the drywall."

"You're *kidding!*"

"Katherine spotted them first," Randy says. "From the landing upstairs. When she called me, I thought maybe she was talking about two or three bees. But there were dozens of them, a big dark clump of them."

"So what are you doing about it?"

"Casey's here. And somebody from Dean's."

In the background is the voice of the project manager from the construction company that built our house. He is talking to the exterminator who has just sprayed bee killer. The echoes of loud voices booming off our walls and pine floors make it sound like a construction site.

"Do they know that my father is dying in there?"

"Yes," Randy says. "That's why they're just spraying and patching the hole for now. They'll come back later to drywall and paint it."

"And how is he? My dad?"

"About the same. Not hungry, not eating much," Randy says. "Definitely sleeping more now that the patch is off."

On my parents' kitchen telephone in Dad's neat printing are the names of the people and businesses whose numbers are programmed into speed dial. Reminders of him taking care of the details of daily life. Outside the window, four stories below, a golfer settles into a stance above his ball on the green. The rest of the foursome is laughing, possibly engaged in a joke as they wait at the golf cart nearby, as if time is not passing and the sunlight will never fade.

"May I help you?"

"I need a dress for a funeral."

This is only partly true. The saleswoman in Saks Petites department doesn't have a clue of my real need. My real need is for her to show concern over who died, to give me the opportunity to say, well, he hasn't died yet, but my father is back in my home in Pennsylvania, in my sunroom, in the *process* of dying. My real need is for her to ask why I'm here in Florida, to give me the chance to share that my sister and I have come to our parents' condo to honor our father's last requests—to bring papers back to him from his safe deposit box and to host a farewell dinner on his behalf for his friends.

My need is to describe the boxes that Pat and I packed yesterday and shipped to Pennsylvania. In the boxes were fall clothes for Mother and Daddy, since they actually came to visit us in Lancaster last May, expecting to be there just for the summer and not for the Fall. That in the boxes we packed a brand new windbreaker of Dad's—still with the tags on it—and his wool-lined raincoat, in case he can go outside again. We also chose a suit for him in which to be laid out. It is a rich black fabric with a reddish sheen. To go with the suit, we chose a white shirt, a black-and-maroon-print tie, and a tie clip in the shape of two criss-crossed golf clubs.

Surely the saleswoman would then be wondering why I am shopping at a time like this, which would give me the chance to explain that my sister and her daughter, Suzanne, who drove here for the day from her home in Stuart, are relaxing at the pool; and that I came here partly to give Pat and Suzanne a chance to visit and partly for practical matters such as, well, there will be no time to shop for a dress once my father dies. Though I have already purchased a suit in Cape Cod, I will need two outfits: one for the viewing and one for the day of the funeral.

"Do you want to wear black?" It seems preposterous that this saleswoman is focused on her job, that *anyone* could be

living her daily routine while everything in my life smacks of
paramount urgency. What does she mean by that: *Do I want
to wear black?*

"I guess so." Perhaps she is trying to ascertain whether I
am a trend follower or a woman who blazes her own trails.
My nerves are dangling on the outside of my body, exposed,
reacting to the slightest touch.

She holds up a dark navy dress, sleeveless, V-neck.

"How about this?" she asks. "I only have one. It's a size
six."

"That's fine," I say. "My size."

"Do you want a jacket to match?"

"Okay."

"I only have a four, an eight, and a twelve."

"I'll try the four."

Our interaction feels hollow, but the dress and jacket fit,
so I buy them. At Tiffany's, a sterling bangle bracelet behind
the display case catches my eye, then a pair of S-shaped earrings. I try them on, but do not ponder; they will be fine.
This is not shopping as usual. There is no entertainment in
perusing and making the selection, scant comfort in treating
myself. Suddenly putting together an outfit is simply a matter
of business: See it, try it, buy it.

The Joan & David store is holding a "Going out of Business" sale. There are no navy blue shoes to match my dress.
But there are strappy black heels, taupe sling-backs, black lin-
en pumps, very nice, all in my size. This is getting confusing.
I buy them all.

The shopping bags dangling from my hands present a
problem: How will I get them home? There isn't one inch
of available space in my suitcase. At Bloomingdale's, suitcases
are sold on the upper level. Lugging another suitcase through
the airport isn't an option: It has to have wheels. There is a

Kipling, a brand I've seen once in a backpack we purchased for Katherine. The suitcase is navy blue, the same color and style as Katherine's backpack. It's twenty-two inches, identical in size to one I already own. It seems wasteful to buy the same size. And at $200! But the others look dull. This is taking too much energy; who cares what it costs? The salesman, a young guy with a crew cut, offers to get a new one from the back. He returns with a black one.

"This one's brand new," he says. "Still has the wrapper on it. Unless you want the navy blue model from the floor."

That's it; I cannot make one more decision. Forget it. Just forget it.

At TJMaxx, on the way back to the condo, there is an army green canvas American Tourister trimmed in fake brown leather. It has wheels. A pull handle. $59.99. Perfect. Sold.

"Where have you two been? I've been trying to get you all day!" It's three o'clock. Marge is crying on the other end of the telephone. I feel guilty admitting that I've been shopping and Pat's been lounging at the pool. "He's getting worse. Hospice asked for the name of the funeral home. He's taking morphine drops every half hour."

My hand feels clammy around the kitchen telephone receiver. Pat is standing three feet away from me looking worried as she listens to me saying *oh no, oh no*.

"He's asking if you two called," she says. We did call on Wednesday, the night we arrived, and twice yesterday. This is Friday. "He wants to know if you're okay. He keeps reaching out and saying, 'Wait, wait!'" Marge is talking nonstop, as if it has been years since we've caught up. "He told Katherine: 'Keep up the good work, Honey.'"

After we hang up, Pat wants to know every word, and now I am the one with tears in my voice. Waiting until Sunday when our flight is scheduled to return home is impossible.

"I want to go back," I say. "Today."

We book a flight out of Fort Lauderdale at 8:20 p.m., the last two seats available. This will give us time to show up at Crystal Lakes, greet our father's friends, and give them his message. We won't have time for dinner ourselves, but a cousin who lives nearby has graciously agreed to stay through the dinner with Dad's friends.

We get dressed and pack. Suzanne helps us to close up the condo. Plastic wrap on the toilet seats to keep the water inside from drying up. Water turned off four stories below with an iron crowbar to reach the underground faucet. Electric switches—except for the air conditioning and one light in the hallway—turned off in the breaker box. Telephone books propping open the refrigerator and dishwasher to keep mold from growing. Thermostat set on air conditioning, seventy-eight degrees.

The condo door behind us is locked, both bolts, but we doublecheck it, as our mother has instructed us to do since we were knee-high. The question of who or when someone will return dashes through my mind, but there's no time now to ponder it.

Reggie Wagaman hands his camera to another guest, positions himself between Pat and me, puts his arms behind our waists. All of us pretend to smile.

Dad's friends have arrived at Crystal Lakes Country Club's lower level. They've come in all shapes and sizes: short and round, tall and lanky, most wearing glasses, some bald, some white-haired. Most are members of Century Village's Board of Directors. Dad guided them through the purchase and transfer of their community's golf course from its developer, a gesture which, to them, is indicative of his generous nature. Their wives and lady friends kiss us on the cheek and call us *Honey*. Their names are offered with handshakes and hugs. With Dad's credit card, Pat has prepaid the dinner, a fixed price buffet plus several bottles of wine, paving the way for us to bolt out of here in time to catch our plane.

It is as if there is a contest being held to determine who can speak most highly of our father. A contest with no prize. *Well respected. Integrity. A gentle man. Always a smile, that incessant warm smile. A heart as big as the day is long.* Pat and I smile and listen to what our father has meant to his friends, an experience that should lift our spirits but only deepens our longing for him. Finally, it is time for us to head to the airport.

"Excuse me." My voice, according to Mother, is too soft for people wearing hearing aids, yet they gather around. We stand in a large circle that seems utterly empty in the center.

"We want to thank you all for coming to celebrate our father's friendship. We wish we could stay, but because Dad's not doing well, my sister and I have booked an earlier flight out of Fort Lauderdale." Around the circle there are heads nodding, eyes warm with sympathy.

"We hope you all enjoy dinner. Before we go, I have a message from my dad to all of you, a message he dictated to me from his bed on August 26th. Then I have a prayer that we found on Dad's bedroom dresser. It's in his handwriting, and it looks like a meal blessing, so we thought we would read that as well."

"Yes, yes," one man says. "Mike always says the blessing before the meal."

"I hope I can get through this," I whisper. The paper is shaking in my hands; I can feel my lips quivering. In my mind is the image of Dad slightly propped on his pillow dictating this message to his friends now gathered around me.

"My wife and I enjoyed all the wonderful years we spent at Century Village and are appreciative of all the many good friends we made while there. I want to wish them God's every blessing and many good years at Century Village."

As Pat and I leave, our parents' friends hug us again and hand us cards to deliver to Dad. By the grace of God, we have fulfilled our father's requests. By the grace of God, we are on our way back to him. A sense of relief mixes with sadness as we climb the stairs to leave Crystal Lakes. The emotion is so overwhelming that to express it might release the dam inside, rendering us incapable of making our way home. So halfway up the stairs—before we reach the front door—Pat leads us toward more practical matters.

"Guess how much that meal was," she says.

"I don't know, how much?"

"$169!" she says. "For eleven people!"

"Including the wine?"

"Including the wine!"

Cars speed past us on Route 95 South. There's less than an hour to get to the airport, return the rental car, catch a shuttle bus, check our bags, and get to the gate. Massive green signs mark each exit and, so far, none of them point to Fort Lauderdale's airport. I am a lousy navigator, a hopeless frustration to any driver. I am easily distracted when Pat brings up the subject of pallbearers.

"Let's see, how many grandsons are there?" she asks.

"Well, there's Anthony, Charles, Michael, Danny, Shawn. Patrick won't come in from England, do you think?"

"Probably not."

"Okay, then Peter makes six."

"We should ask our cousin Michael, too ... "

"And Johnny. Do you think it would be okay to have eight of them?"

"I guess so."

And suddenly we are wondering if we missed the exit.

"The map says Exit 26A! There is no 26A!"

"Just tell me where to get off," Pat insists.

She is driving faster than my mind can think.

"I hate reading maps!"

"Should I get off here?" Pat pushes. "Hurry up!"

"I don't know!" Then because a decision is required, I make one. "Yes, go ahead!"

We take the exit and there, off the ramp, is a gift from God: a gas station.

Pat asks the attendant how to get to the Fort Lauderdale airport. He points straight ahead.

"That way," he says.

"How far?" The thundering of our hearts is almost audible.

The gas station attendant smiles. "Oh, about two minutes."

Dad has always been emphatic about arriving ahead of time. When we were young, if he told us we were leaving at 7:00 to go somewhere, we learned to be ready by 6:40 because, without fail, that's when he'd holler for all of us to pile into the car. It was not acceptable to merely comply with the timetable; doing so would mean hearing Dad chastise, "What took you so long?" He showed up early for doctor appointments, meetings, and even earlier when getting a good seat mattered to him. After he and Mother moved to Florida, they arrived at church by 3:15 p.m. on Saturdays for four o'clock mass. When visiting, this drove us mad, cutting into an afternoon of basking in the Florida sun just for a prime parking space in the St. Ambrose lot. We used to joke that if he could, Dad would get to his own funeral early.

Now here we are, desperate to return to him in time. At the airport, the plane is delayed. First, one hour. Then two hours. *Please, Dad, please, please, please, don't leave without us.*

The delay gives us time for dinner. Nothing looks appetizing in the airport cafe. I can hardly think of food, but this may be our only opportunity to eat. I buy a cookie, take a bite, throw it away. We return to the gate, and there is another announcement. Another delay. At a nearby stand, I purchase a piece of pizza, take a bite, throw it away.

We try to read, but neither of us feels like reading. We could talk the time away, but there is nothing left to say. We call home; Dad is sleeping. We call home again; Dad is resting. And again; Dad took a sip of Gatorade. And again; Dad is waiting for us.

Finally, on the plane, it is almost midnight. The passengers look bleary-eyed; some of them doze. In the end seat across the aisle from me, Pat is reading, then she stares straight ahead. The pen in my hand fills the empty pages of my spiral-bound tablet. It takes on a life of its own, recounting my escapade at safe deposit box #447, my shopping trip at Towne Center, the bittersweetness of meeting Dad's friends.

In the spotlight of the overhead bulb, the pen takes me into uncharted waters. It writes words to speak in Dad's memory at a funeral that I can hardly bear to think about. It is as if the pen takes charge so I don't have to. It writes and writes and writes.

Three years ago, Dad hosted a farewell dinner, as he and my mother prepared to move from Pittsburgh and make Century Village in Deerfield Beach their full-time home. At that dinner, my sisters and I and our families presented our parents with a "Memory Book" that captured some of the moments each of us had cherished with Mother and Dad. It seems appropriate, now that Dad has moved again—this time to his heavenly home—to recall just a few of those memories that made Dad our loving and well loved father and grandfather.

Peter remembered their walks around the reservoir and his grandpap speeding up their car trips by turning a few red lights to

*green just by pointing at them. Shawn said, "Grandpap is the man
we all wish we could be. He would always make big problems seem
so small. I look up to him because he was never too busy to listen."
Suzanne remembered sailing in The Gateway Clipper down the
Monongohela with her grandfather, playing gin rummy and shuffle-
board with him and watching him shoot an awesome game of pool.
Randy remembered playing golf with Dad as "the nicest four hours
of golf imaginable. I could hit every ball in the water, the trees, the
traps, yet when I get back in the golf cart, everything is okay; Dad
has this effect on everyone. I always feel the next drive is going to be
a killer followed by a simple chip to within three feet of the pin for a
birdie putt." Michael remembered his great grandpap magically pulling quarters from behind his ear. . . .*

The tablet is almost full. The pen writes on the backs of
sheets now, up the margins of the pages willy-nilly, wherever
there is space. The pages are out of order, but the pen does
not care. It cannot stop writing. It *has* to write.

Until finally, ever so politely, the pen stops. It stops and
rests on the tablet, giving me the chance just to sit. In my
tiredness, it feels as if someone is cradling me. As if God is
wrapping me in peace. Helping me to breathe. Breathe.
Breathe.

And finally here we are—Pat and I—in my sunroom at
Dad's bedside. It is 3:40 a.m. Saturday. Dad is sound asleep. In
the corner of the room, a lamp is lit next to the night nurse.
Pat stands on one side of Dad; on the other, I lean over and
feel the warmth of his arm.

"Daddy," I whisper. "We're back."

He opens his eyes, confused. Then he smiles.

"Oh, hi," he says.

"We met your friends," I say.

"They all send their love," Pat says.

"I wish we could have bottled it up and brought it back
to you."

The corners of his mouth turn up.

"And we got everything from the safe deposit box," Pat adds.

"We can go over it in the morning," Dad says.

Pat and I nod. "Yes."

Dad smiles again, closes his eyes, goes back to sleep.

The voice of the night nurse is gentle.

"You can see the weight lifted from his shoulders," she says. "He's been waiting for the two of you. You can see the weight lifted now that you're here."

10

All the Difference in the World

Dad opens his eyes; their focus is drifting away. Marge offers him Gatorade to moisten his lips. He nods, then musters the strength to sip through a straw. The liquid rises slowly toward his mouth, as do our hopes that it will make it there, that our father will be granted the dignity of at least this minute accomplishment. His appetite has dwindled away, and the hospice people have advised us not to force food on him. For the most part, Katherine's been playing outside, visiting friends, or at gymnastics practice. Now she stands near the bed and touches her grandfather's hand. He opens his eyes and sees her there.

"Hi, Grandpap," she says.

The sides of my father's lips curl slightly.

"Hi, Honey," he whispers. Another act of strength.

Marge and I join Katherine around Dad's bed and attempt to conjure up family memories, a suggestion on the hospice family tip sheet. It is a strenuous endeavor when what we really want to do is rest our heads on his chest and cry.

"Remember the Coco-Cammerata picnics?" Marge says to me.

"Yes." I nod for her to continue.

Marge looks at Katherine. "These were family reunions we had a long time ago with relatives of both of Grandpap's parents. Dozens of them."

This memory has been shared often, but Dad would relish the thought of his stories being passed on. Marge continues addressing Katherine so that Dad can hear.

"Well, we used to have these egg toss contests. Grandpap would team up with Aunt Lena. He'd slip a hard-boiled egg from his pocket and switch it with the raw egg. As the game progressed, and everyone stepped farther and farther back from their partners, Grandpap and Aunt Lena were still in the game, tossing their egg back and forth until somebody noticed that when their egg fell and smacked against the ground, it didn't splatter the way the other eggs did. Someone would holler, 'Not fair!' and Grandpap would throw his head back and laugh."

Now we laugh, too, and then there is silence.

Is Marge wracking her brain, as I am, for something, *anything*, to say?

Pat comes to the door of the sunroom and whispers. "You're supposed to be talking about things he might enjoy. Memories. That's what the hospice paper says."

Marge looks at me and rolls her eyes.

"Would you like to suggest something?" I ask through my teeth.

Each of us in our own way tries to guess what Dad may need. Marge gives him medicine through a dropper. Pat cools his forehead with a damp washcloth. Dad's youngest brother, Johnny, has made the 4-hour drive from Pittsburgh with his wife, Marie, to visit. Through the French doors, the two brothers look like a Norman Rockwell painting: Uncle Johnny seated at Dad's bedside, elbows on his knees, hands folded, uncharacteristically quiet, with the slightest hint of hope in his eyes. There is none of the wry Maxwell Smart humor that typically emanates from our uncle. Instead his presence next to our father is steadfast. The expression on his face says, *I will do anything for my brother, anything, just name it.* And so he sits for hours waiting for the word: a drink, a taste of Jell-O, a pillow to be propped, until one of us gently nudges Uncle Johnny to come and get a bite to eat.

Our cousins arrive from Pittsburgh. Together we eat my friend Peg's homemade chili and tiramisu or sandwiches delivered from Isaac's. Family members weave in and out of the sunroom, the dining room, the kitchen, the family room.

In the privacy of the screened porch, one cousin gives my sisters and me an overview of the practicalities that our father's death will necessitate. His own father passed away eight years ago, then his mother, and he has acquired first-hand knowledge of such matters. He has brought with him a white ruled sheet of twenty-some items we need to think about or to which we must find answers. The way Mother and Dad's condo is titled. The question of power of attorney. The status of quarterly tax payments.

When we were young, our band of cousins never anticipated such gruesome tasks. We were too engrossed in the diversions of Sunday visits to our Grandma and Grandpap Coco's house on Mount Royal Boulevard. Behind the house, wooden planks wobbled beneath our feet as we tried to keep our balance between the rows of Grandpap's garden: tomato plants, green peppers, eggplant, all lush and viney. Grandpap would yank green onions from the ground, then clean them against his apron. He taunted us with the onions, brushing them against our faces.

"*Vieni mangiare!*" he insisted. "Come on, taste."

We tried to escape his relentless coaxing, but sooner or later the pungent taste was on every tongue, the odor in all of our mouths.

"*Nice-a girl!*" Our grandfather threw back his head and laughed at the sour looks on our faces. "*Nice-a boy!* Put hair on your chest!"

Now here we are, like those kids facing long-stemmed green onions, trying to fend them off, the more experienced knowing the bitterness yet to be tasted by the others. My sisters and I are in awe of the list our cousin has composed, grateful for his thoughtfulness. Another cousin offers to compile a list of Dad's business associations and accomplishments, so we will have them for writing the obituary.

Others come to call, too, each bringing his or her own brand of love. It illuminates the reasons God created families. It makes me remember the mountains we climbed together as youngsters, feeling strong enough to topple dead trees, the childhood games we played on our grandmother's steps, the wooded trails we hiked, the holiday feasts we shared. It's as if they were all training grounds, bonding exercises for a time of even greater importance that only God imagined.

There is warmth in the September sun shining on us here in the screened porch. Freshness and power and warmth.

"Dad, would you like me to read to you?"

His eyes are closed, but he nods.

"I have Norman Vincent Peale's book right here. *The Power of Positive Thinking.* Remember when you used to read it to me?"

Again he nods.

"Would you like me to read it to you?"

"Yes," he says.

Amazing. Norman Vincent Peale in my sunroom. It was the book we studied in Ruth Group this summer. A wave of warmth runs through me. How tender God is! How precise his orchestration in getting this very book in my hands at this very moment.

Chapter One, "Believe in Yourself." At first, this feels awkward. I have never before read to my father. But as we move through the paragraphs, the words recapture a long-ago connection between my father and me. It is the completion of a circle. A line with no end. I read until my mouth is dry, my throat hoarse. Is he listening? Can he hear? Beneath these words is a familiar energy to which I cling, a small girl holding her father's hand.

"If God be for us, who can be against us? That's a Bible verse, Romans 8:31."

Dad's eyes blink open.

"I like that." It is the first he's spoken since I started reading. His voice is raspy. "If God be for us, who can be against us?" he repeats.

"Yes," I say. "It's true, isn't it?"

"Yes."

"I'm glad you're here, Dad," I tell him. "I'm glad you came to our house."

"It makes all the difference in the world," he says.

Today is Labor Day. One by one, those who traveled a distance say goodbye, leaving to return to work tomorrow. I have always dreaded family departures from my home, yearned for my relatives to stay for one more cup of tea, one more chat into the night. Soon it will just be Randy, Katherine, Mother, and me, along with the on-duty nurse, alone in our house with Dad. It is hard to watch them leave, knowing how our lives will have changed by the next time we see each other.

After they are gone, Katherine visits her grandfather's bedside, and there she is four years old again at the end of a visit she and I made to my parents in Florida. The week belonged to the two of them: Katherine and my father. Together they had collected seashells on the beach, visited and revisited the dozens of stray cats populating a nearby park, made friends with the elephant at Lion Country Safari, cruised on the *Jungle Queen*, filled up on ice cream. Having hugged my parents goodbye, we were waiting to board our plane at the West Palm Beach airport. From behind the gate, my father smiled and waved to my daughter, who was holding my hand. Huge alligator-sized tears streamed down Katherine's cheeks, tears of utter longing.

"Would you like to give Grandpap one more hug?" I offered.

She nodded, then ran from the boarding line back to her grandfather. As though his cardiologist had never cautioned him against lifting, he swooped her up in his arms, and she buried her face in his shoulder. There was such unencumbered love between the two of them, a child and her grandfather. If only there were a way to leave her with him and take her with me at the same time.

Now Katherine leans over her grandfather's bedside and touches his arm. She's wearing pink and green rosebud pajamas and slippers that are shaped like frogs.

"Goodnight, Grandpap," she whispers.

"Goodnight, Sweetheart," he says.

I awaken in the middle of the night, and the echo of the oxygen concentrator against the pine floorboards reminds me that Dad is here. For that, I am grateful. I slip on my robe and slippers, tiptoe downstairs. The night nurse, a magazine on her lap, reads by the dim lamp in the corner of the sunroom.

"Hi, Daddy," I say. I take his hand and he opens his eyes, turns his head toward me, smiles. It is quiet and dark and still. In the middle of the night, thoughts occur to me that have pulled me downstairs, words I would not want to leave unspoken.

When you see God, please thank him for me; he gave me the best father on earth.

And, *I love you, Dad.*

And, *Thank you for everything, Dad.*

Somewhere I have read that to free the dying to move on, the living must let go.

So early on the morning of Wednesday, September 6, I tell my father how much we are going to miss him. And that it's okay for him to move on to be with Jesus. In fact, it's wonderful, I say.

On this very day, Katherine wakes up for school feeling out of sorts. This is not the little girl who cartwheels her way into the kitchen each morning for breakfast. Dressed for school, she stands quietly next to her bed.

"This is the worst day of my whole life," she tells me.

"Oh, I'm so sorry, honey," I say. "Do you want to talk about it?"

"No."

"Sometimes it makes you feel a little better to talk about things."

"I don't want to," she says.

"Okay, but let me know if you change your mind."

Recently my sister Pat, an elementary school principal, had suggested that I call Katherine's new third grade teacher to advise her of what's going on at our home. It might help her to know, she said, just in case Katherine acts it out in some way in class. It sounded like a good idea, one on which I'd meant to follow through, but I never got around to looking up Mrs. Quinn's home telephone number. Then last week, several days after the school year began, Mrs. Quinn called me at home. When her name and telephone number appeared on our Caller ID, I was incredulous. *What? Now God is looking up telephone numbers for me?* Mrs. Quinn's voice was gentle and sweet.

"I don't know Katherine well yet," she said, "but I wondered if something is wrong. If she's having difficulty adjusting to me or to third grade for some reason."

Grateful for her sensitivity, I could have reached through the telephone receiver and hugged her.

"She seems okay when she's out on the playground with her friends," she continued, "but in class—during story time, for example—while the other children are giggling and enjoying themselves, Katherine seems far away, almost sullen."

It made me heartsick to hear the word "sullen" applied to the little girl we often call "Happy Head."

Now at her bedroom door, I turn and face her.

"It's been hard with Grandpap being sick, hasn't it?" I say.

She nods.

"Ever since Grandpap's been sick," she says, "I can't stand it when things go wrong, even little things that don't usually bother me that much. Like when there are knots in my hair."

"I know what you mean," I say. I tell her about my trip to the dry cleaners soon after my sister Dee had died. When the dry cleaner told me my clothes weren't ready on time, I left the building and burst into tears.

"Really?"

"Yes," I assure her. "It's hard when somebody you love dies."

In the past, we have discussed the broad spiritual aspects of a person's dying, but now she is curious about the logistics. So we talk about the undertaker who will come to take her grandfather's body and drive it to Pittsburgh for the funeral. About the trip that we'll all take to Pittsburgh, about the viewing where relatives and friends she didn't even know she had will come and pay their last respects to her grandfather. About the funeral and about the mausoleum where his body will rest close to those of his brothers and other relatives.

Later downstairs, Katherine helps herself to a Pop-tart before leaving for school. She isn't doing her usual hand-stands or gushing over the cat, but there is a sense of peace about her.

"It did help to talk about it," she admits. "I feel better."

She walks down the flagstone path and cuts through our backyard toward the bus stop. At the French doors where I'm left standing, her first words that morning replay themselves in my mind: "This is the worst day of my whole life."

Jody stops in around ten o'clock. She spends time alone with Dad and with the day nurse. In the foyer, as she is leaving, her eyes are filled with sorrow.

"We think that he will probably go within the next twenty-four hours," she says.

"Twenty-four hours," I repeat.

"Twenty-four or thirty-six."

"How can you tell?" Suddenly it strikes me as an odd skill to have, this intimate familiarity with death. Jody talks about the color of Dad's skin, the coldness of his feet, the yellow around his fingernails.

"Should I call my sister?" I ask.

"When was she planning to come?"

"Right after work, around four or four-thirty."

"That should be okay," Jody says. "Are you going to be all right?"

I nod, though I am no longer sure how to determine all rightness.

"Call if you need anything," she offers.

At Dad's side, it is calm and peaceful.

"Dad, when you get to heaven, will you let us know that you're okay?"

He does not respond. Has he heard me? Why is he holding on? Is there something we've forgotten to do? Something left unfinished?

I wonder if he thinks about what will happen to Mother after he goes, an issue with which we've been wrestling in our own minds. What does Dad want for her? Where does he see her living? We've been hesitant to ask for fear that he will say he hopes she can live with one of us, an arrangement that simply would not work—for her or for us. The other day, Dad told Pat that Mother could be a big help to me.

"What did he mean by that?" I asked.

"I don't know," Pat said. "I guess that Mother can help you with laundry and with watching Katherine."

"Was he insinuating that she should live with me?"

"No, not at all," Pat said.

Perhaps it was his way of expressing hope that she would move up north to live *near* us. This actually *has* been the plan we've discussed loosely with Mother, getting her an apartment in Lancaster near Pat and me, a plan with which she has nodded in agreement. We do not know what it will be like for our mother, nearly deaf, living alone after sixty-nine years of dependency upon our father. In the privacy of out-of-the-way rooms or over the telephone, my sisters and I have talked endlessly about this.

"Don't worry about Mother," I offer Dad now. "We will take care of her."

Again, no response.

Knowing Dad, there might be something of a practical nature requiring attention. One of the issues concerning him during the delayed delivery of his car was that the paperwork for his quarterly estimated income tax—due June 15—was in the trunk of his car. If the car didn't arrive on time, he repeatedly mentioned, he would have to visit an IRS office for new forms, which in the end, he did indeed do. Suddenly it occurs to me that the end of another quarter—requiring another estimated tax filing—will arrive next week!

And in his briefcase, there they are: the quarterly tax forms, his checkbook and a U.S. postal return receipt already completed (he is *so* organized!) for the mailing of the tax. It may be the Holy Spirit guiding me, or perhaps I am losing my mind; either way, it seems imperative to write the check, have Mother sign it, and take it to the post office to file their quarterly estimated income taxes.

The traffic on Lititz Pike is not a problem. In fact, I believe that people are going about their routines at a regular clip. After being in the house for so long, it did not occur to me that people were still driving to Stauffer's for groceries, still filling car tanks with gas, still stopping by the Beverage Corral for a six-pack. While I am out, I might as well dash through the drive-up window at Foto Fast, where I dropped off film for processing some time ago.

In line ahead of me is a green station wagon. The driver of the station wagon lingers at the pickup window, oblivious to anyone behind her. My fingers begin tapping against the steering wheel. What is she doing? Why can't she drop off her film or grab her photos and move on? What could possibly warrant this much conversation with the Foto Fast clerk? In the rearview mirror, a beat-up white pick-up truck appears, hugging close to my bumper. The thought of waiting in line for another minute renders me claustrophobic. My shoulders go limp. *Get me out of here. Please, please get me out of here.*

Finally, back at Dad's side, I am breathless.

"Daddy, I mailed your estimated tax payment for September 15th. I sent it 'Return Receipt Requested' just as you always do."

He does not respond. Tears burn my eyes, seeing my father's face, so quiet, so still.

He once described to me how in his early days as a bricklayer, he would build a wall "… one brick at a time. I'd just
take it one brick at a time," he said, "making sure each one
was laid properly. At the end of the day, I would stand back
and admire my work. It just filled me with a sense of accomplishment—doing the job right." If one brick was askew, my
father would tear down the wall and start again, still smooth-
ing on mortar well into dusk.

The parish visitor, a nurse, has come from the Catholic
church Mother and Dad have been attending in Lancaster
this summer. She is a wiry woman in her late forties with
straight brown hair, brown eyes, large teeth. Last month she
visited Dad in the hospital and learned of his intense cramp-
ing.

"I hope it's just kidney stones," she said matter-of-factly.
Her comment made me wince, remembering the excruciating pain of passing kidney stones Dad had once described.
Now the same parish visitor stands across Dad's bed from
me with my mother at her side. My mother trusts all things
Catholic; I am feeling uneasy about this woman's presence.
She has brought communion which Dad's body, all but
shut down now, is incapable of receiving, so she touches his
mouth with it, says a prayer. Then, still standing at Dad's bedside, still within my father's earshot, she looks across the bed
at me.

"What will your mother do afterwards?" she asks. "Will
she move up here?"

My face burns with astonishment. It takes all my strength
not to lash out at her utter insensitivity. But at this point,
what good would it do?

"Yes," I acquiesce.

"With you?"

I can feel my teeth grinding. "No. We'll probably get her a one-bedroom apartment."

And there it is, out in the open: the issue we've avoided discussing with Dad. Could this be the question he's been waiting to have answered? No matter what the bumps along their road, my mother and father have always taken care of one another, always seeing to it that the other had what was needed.

Less than an hour later, a laptop computer perched in front of me on the sunroom sofa, the information sent by my cousin is melding its way into the shape of my father's obituary. One by one, his accomplishments appear on the screen: Board member, National Legislative Committee, Associated Contractors of America. Past President, Pittsburgh Builders Exchange. Board of Directors, Master Builders' Association of Western Pennsylvania. Pennsylvania District Governor, Kiwanis Club. Arbitrator, National Association of Securities Dealers and the American Arbitration Association....

Just beyond my laptop screen is the man responsible for these achievements, his eyes closed, his work finished. In the chair next to him is my husband, quiet and still. The hospice nurse sits in the corner with a magazine on her lap.

Amid the clicking of my laptop keys, Dad's hand inches toward the bed rail. On his more energetic days, he rattled the bed rail as an indication that he needed help using the bedside commode. Immediately, I stand and leave the room, a dignity we have been able to afford my father since Randy or a hospice nurse have been available to help him.

In the kitchen, Mother has her back toward me. Even as her husband draws his final breaths, she stands at the stove stirring the sauce as if grief can be swirled away. How limited I am in knowing what she feels—or even in knowing who she is, for that matter. Who can really know her parents—

their deepest fears, their unmet longings—without having lived their lives? We can take stabs at it, sometimes even hover near the truth, but then we must stand back and realize this: We are not God; we are not their Creator. And even if we were given one tiny glimpse of them the way God sees them, certainly their flaws would remain, but merely as scars from a hidden hurt revealed by the light of the endless love of their Creator, the only one whose vision is flawless.

This I do know about my mother: She has funneled her love to us in the best way that she knows how—cooking our meals, keeping our clothes clean. As all of us grew, and waistlines or vegetarian diets took precedence over her homemade *bracciole* and pasta ricotta, she must have felt her usefulness diminished or, worse yet, her love rejected. I wonder if this very theme is the substance of the invisible wall around her. If being sent away as a child to live with a sister was only the start of a lifetime of being pushed out, made to feel unimportant. Look at her stirring that pot, quietly, alone, as if etched on her heart are the words of Jesus: "If anyone wants to be first, he must be the very last, and the servant of all."

The clock says three: soon Katherine will arrive home from school. A shuffling sound emanates from the sunroom, muffled voices. Then Randy steps into the hallway.

"Hon, come quick!" he says.

"Should I bring my mother?" From the expression on Randy's face, I know.

In the back seat of the metallic red station wagon, Katherine fiddles with a new portable radio. My sister Pat had the presence of mind to bring the radio, a gift for Katherine, when she hurried to our house this afternoon. Darkness is settling in; it is almost eight o'clock on the day of my father's death. Katherine and I are on our way to Payless Shoes, because tomorrow morning we will leave for Pittsburgh; and in packing for the funeral, we found that her dress shoes are too small, and she needs a new pair. We are driving down Fruitville Pike with no pressing reason to return home. Not that the house is empty, but it seems hollow now, nothing anchoring it down.

For the most part, Katherine's radio is a box of static, probably tuned in to AM, for as she scans the airwaves, there is minimal channel selection. Finally, the voice of what sounds like a Baptist minister comes booming through the static.

"And the Lord sent his angels in chariots to get him!" the voice bellows.

"Mommy!" Katherine says. "Did you hear that?"

Though I am in a daze, the words break through to my brain: *And the Lord sent his angels in chariots to get him!*

Images of angels take flight in my mind, dozens of them. My sister Lena waving heaven's activities schedule, squealing in delight. Dee reaching out, her hand cured of psoriasis, her body whole and curvaceous again. Nonno in his gray woolen cap, a twinkle in his eye, still full of fun. Uncle Carmel out front, his eyebrows knitted in feigned impatience, *What took you so long?* And there in the rear are my father's mother and father: the short, solid woman with a gray bun and the wiry Italian laughing now, tickled to see his son. Neither is wearing the apron that tied them to their store. They are lounging in their seats, relaxing at long last, enjoying the ride. The ride. The ride. The perfect way to beckon my father: the thrill of the ride!

And the Lord sent his angels in chariots to get him!

Katherine's voice snaps me out of my reverie. "Mommy, that sounds like what happened at our house today!" she says.

"Oh, Honey, do you know that just this morning I asked Grandpap to somehow let us know when he got to heaven that he was okay?"

"Wow!" she says from the backseat. "He sure got back to us fast!" Her words make me smile, but then it hits me. Who but God would use the voice of a child to deliver such a powerful message? My grip loosens on the steering wheel. I am breathless.

Sometimes in my sunroom, the grace of God is so palpable that I cannot entertain the notion of sitting elsewhere. So I read here. And I pray here. And I write here. I cannot help thinking about the gift God gave me. A whole summer with Dad. A summer to say goodbye.

What was it like? I wonder. I mean for Dad, his dying. Did a messenger of God come to him the way his Pop showed up that day in Cincinnati to fetch his runaway son?

"Come on," his father said.

I remember Dad telling me he was never so glad to see anyone in his life. Could the final surrender have been that lovely?

Today, it just happens, is May 25th, exactly one year since Mother and Dad arrived from Florida for the summer. There it is penciled on last year's calendar page, Thursday, May 25: *USAir Flight #115. Lv. Fort Laud. 2:05 p.m. Ar. Pgh. 4:42 p.m. Flight #4428. Lv. Pgh. 5:20 p.m. Ar. Lanc. 6:25 p.m. Mother & Dad arrive.*

Mother is getting ready to move for the third time since Dad passed on. The apartment was too burdensome for her, assisted living too confining. This time she is moving to a new one-bedroom unit at a nearby retirement community. We have sold the Florida condo. We have had Mother fitted with two digital hearing aids, giving us all, for the first time in many years, the opportunity to hold conversations with her. I do not know if she will ever fully understand us, or us her for that matter, but we are trying.

We have made it through a cold, barren winter, and this is what Spring brings to my sunroom. Through the windows, the dogwood is in full bloom again; the leaves on the hollyhocks are magnificent, a cluster of wide-open hands. The ceiling fan is still. The walls have been painted with a fresh coat of Seacliff Beige, the trim a bright white. The wicker settee sits against the wall again, where the Hospice bed once stood, under the Bart Forbes print of an Amish lady in a crisp, white bonnet. The grandmother's clock has just chimed eleven. On this peaceful May morning, my sunroom is filled with books and sunlight and the lush, grainy shadows of Armstrong pines forever growing heavenward on the other side of the window.

Epilogue

There was no choir at St. Scholastica, the church where I grew up. Or maybe there was, and I didn't hear it. My father's singing surrounded me, a cushion against which to lean. Even now, I close my eyes and there is the firmness of that voice belting out a hymn: sure, insistent. It was a robustness that came from a place deep in his heart, a heart so big that its song echoed high into the rafters.

Dad's sanctuary extended far beyond the church. In fact, it had no limits. He would take us cruising along the Fort Lauderdale canal aboard the *Jungle Queen* en route to the Seminole Indian Village, the waterfront homes aglow with white twinkle lights. At the captain's very mention of "Let Me Call You Sweetheart," Dad would burst into song until the other passengers couldn't help but join in, his singing as clear as the lights glimmering on the water. Or at Lancaster's American Music Theater, his voice soared to accompany the chorus, not that the audience was invited to sing along, but the old Broadway hits were too rich for my father to resist.

This is the voice I still hear today, even though my father is gone. A voice that is firm, sure, a beat ahead of the others. A voice that insists, that leaves little room for doubt, that cannot be ignored. It is there when I embark with trepidation on a new endeavor, such as writing a book. *You can do it. Go ahead. Anything you put your mind to, you can do.* It is there at my daughter's bedside as I gaze into her sleeping face. *Smart girl. Doesn't miss a trick, does she?* And then in the church pew, the organ music climbs to a crescendo. Can it be? Can a voice really carry that far? It embraces me. It penetrates my skin, touches my heart. And I am safe.

NOTES

[1] Lewis, C.S. *Mere Christianity*. New York: HarperCollins ed., 2001.

[2] Peale, Norman Vincent. *The Power of Positive Thinking*. Fifth Ed. New York: Ballantine, 1996.

[3] *Life Application Study Bible*. New International Version. Wheaton, Illinois: Tyndale House. Grand Rapids, Michigan: Zondervan, 1991.

[4] Minot, Susan. *Evening*. New York: Random House, 1998.

[5] *Life Application Study Bible*. New International Version. Wheaton, Illinois: Tyndale House. Grand Rapids, Michigan: Zondervan, 1991.

[6] Callanan, Maggie and Kelley, Patricia. *Final Gifts*. New York: Simon & Schuster, 1992.

About the Author

Jan Groft holds an MFA in Writing from Vermont College. She has taught creative nonfiction writing and authored essays, short fiction, and articles appearing in *Northeast*, *Habersham Review*, *Voices in Italian Americana*, and *Entrepreneur*. Formerly president and creative director of an advertising agency that she founded in 1980, she has garnered numerous awards for creative excellence, including the CLIO award. She lives in Lititz, Pennsylvania.